FAST >> FORWARD

HOW TO TURBO-CHARGE BUSINESS, SALES, AND CAREER GROWTH

SCOTT STEINBERG
WWW.AKEYNOTESPEAKER.COM

PUBLISHED BY:
BLUEPRINT: YOUR NEW ROADMAP
TO SUCCESS™

FAST >> FORWARD

1ST EDITION
© 2020 HOW MEDIA LLC

EDITED BY DAMON BROWN
OF DAMONBROWN.NET

DEDICATION

FOR T + Z – A CONSTANT SOURCE OF INSPIRATION, WORKING TIRELESSLY TO HELP US CREATE A BRIGHTER TOMORROW TODAY.

>>FAST FORWARD>>
TABLE OF CONTENTS

DISRUPTING YOURSELF: TAKING A MORE FORWARD-THINKING APPROACH TO LEADERSHIP

BEING UPWARDLY MOBILE: PUTTING YOUR CAREER ON THE FAST-TRACK

GROWTH IS NEVER BY MERE CHANCE. IT IS THE RESULT OF FORCES WORKING TOGETHER.

- JAMES CASH PENNY

A GOOD PLAN, VIOLENTLY EXECUTED NOW, IS BETTER THAN A PERFECT PLAN NEXT WEEK.

- GEN. GEORGE S. PATTON

>>INTRO

Everything we know about business is wrong.

Contrary to popular opinion, it doesn't take 10,000 hours to become a leading expert; 40 years to retire rich; or $1 billion to build the next Slack or Twitter. What if, from a personal standpoint, you could go from being broke to traveling the world first-class in less time than it takes peers to graduate from college – or from intern to CEO of an organization overnight? Likewise, as a business leader, how much of a difference would it make to your enterprise if you could create products, services, and solutions that legions of raving fans adore without having to spend years tied up in research and development... or burning through millions in startup capital? The more you learn to apply the principles contained here in *FAST>>FORWARD* – including **F.A.S.T.E.R.**, a simple formula for accelerating personal and professional growth or building and sustaining competitive advantage – the sooner you'll be able to achieve major milestones in your career and business.

Like the most important concepts in life, **F.A.S.T.E.R.** – which reminds us that the more insights and resources you can bring to bear to solve a problem, the more successfully you can multiply the speed at which you can tackle it – is simple to learn, difficult to master. It breaks down as follows:

1. F – Focus – Study a problem closely, learning everything you can about the challenge before you.

2. A – Analyze – Assess potential approaches you can take to solve this dilemma and potential resources you'll need to accomplish the task.

3. S – Strategize – Weigh possible risks and rewards associated with each angle of attack. Then, given the above insights, determine which strategies for moving forward are most practical and favorable, and develop an action plan and steps you need to take to achieve your goal.

4. T – Turbo-Charge – Seek out and apply time- and effort-saving tools, technologies, and techniques that can help you streamline your methodology, speed up its execution, and minimize the costs (both in terms of finances and opportunity) required to deploy it.

5. E – Execute – Engage and put your strategic plan into action.

6. R – Revise – Review the results of your efforts and use the insights gained to enhance and improve future tactics – or pivot to a more effective approach.

For example: Leading social network Facebook currently serves over 2 billion people worldwide today, who exchange more than 100 billion messages every day. But circa 2008, like many other self-made upstarts, it was a scrappy young startup that was strapped for time and resources, and offered its site in English only. With 60% of its user base living outside of America, it needed to find a way to quickly scale and internationalize to serve foreign audiences. Rather than invest in professional translation services, which could be slow and costly to implement though, the company instead opened the process of translating its website to its 69 million users, who could suggest and vote on which user-generated translations to implement. Within just *24 hours*, the site had been translated into French with the help of 4000 native speakers – and within 24 months, the site had expanded to 74 languages worldwide.

Believe it or not, the formula really is that simple. In fact, most of us already apply steps one, five, and six in our lives. We naturally gravitate towards the business opportunities and career paths that appear the most promising. But trouble comes when we overlook steps two, three, and four (*Analyze, Strategize, and Turbo-Charge*) – the *accelerants* that can help take us from zero to 100 in record time – as we default to common assumptions and overlook the wise shortcuts that can help us leapfrog challenges or sidestep them entirely. Think of these accelerants as fuel for your professional fires: All it takes is for you to light a simple spark of inspiration to watch them ignite and send your prospects soaring.

For instance, when I was a newly-minted college graduate without a journalism degree, I could have spent years applying to newsrooms across America and competing with thousands of smarter and/ or better-qualified candidates in hopes of getting hired. Instead, I decided to leapfrog over the line by looking for emerging areas where the market lacked authoritative voices and starting a website covering high-tech products and video games to help me build a work portfolio and boost my visibility, just as the high-tech field (and high-tech gadgets) began to capture the mainstream public's imagination. Shortly afterward, I used then-new search engines and social networks to identify entertainment and pop culture editors who might be looking for writers. A few dozen emails later, I had a column for *The Los Angeles Times* at age 21, thousands of regular readers, and the beginnings of a burgeoning freelance career. Thanks to the magic of these accelerants, it would quickly balloon to 600+ outlets and regular appearances from CNN to *Rolling Stone*, despite the fact I possessed little to no prior professional writing experience.

Likewise, applying a similar approach to attacking the challenge of product development, and taking a contrarian stance on business strategy, can also help companies put themselves on the fast-track to success. Case in point: According to Crunchbase, nearly $19 billion in venture capital was invested across more than 25,000 startups between Q2 2018 and Q2 2019 alone – including thousands of software companies who raised an average of $40 million per seed round. But for all the time such firms spend creating forward-thinking solutions, most of these online app developers' fortunes ultimately depend on simple, easily experimented-with variables, like whether or not a customer will ultimately click or tap to download and use their cutting-edge products.

All of which begs the question: Why spend years of time developing such grand-scale ventures when you could instead gauge their viability just by putting up a $20 website template touting the same product's features (along with mock-up screenshots) first and – before ever spending millions creating the software solution itself – seeing if you could instead actually get anyone to tap or click on the download button? Once you'd perfected the art of attracting and converting customers; getting a sense of which solutions and features most resonated with them; and determined just how big the potential audience for the software product would be (and gotten a better idea of precisely how much to spend making it, based on this information) – *that* would then be the time to start doubling-down on product development. Strangely, although even many entrepreneurs still don't think this way today, it's a simple, straightforward approach to right-sizing business solutions and strategies that popular online crowdfunding sites like Kickstarter and Indiegogo have proven the viability of a thousand times over.

Bottom line: Who says you have to take great risks to earn great rewards, or can't count your chickens before they've hatched? What makes you certain there's not a shorter path from here to there as you go about the process of navigating the roadmap of professional success? Heck, we've personally used similar strategies – creating promotions before final products, using audience responses to outreach campaigns to gauge impact, and leveraging each of these tools to secure the funding needed to ultimately build these projects – to flip basic business models on their head, de-risk new ventures, and go from idea to result much faster. In fact, a software company using such strategies to create small product demos, snap screenshots, put up website pages, engage in promotional activities, and use pre-orders generated as a result of these efforts to fund future development before the solution even ships is often one better-poised to succeed than an unproven gamble, no matter how well-funded or venture-capital-backed.

Facing a huge problem you can't seem to solve at work? Worried you've plateaued on the job? Wondering what it takes to come up with your organization's next big breakthrough idea when time, money, and resources are tighter than ever? Fear not: Within the pages of this book, you'll meet a host of individuals and organizations who found ways to catapult themselves from zero to hero, and wannabe to winner, in no time flat. From more forward-thinking approaches to leadership strategy to simple ways to leverage technology and customer experiences to create competitive advantage, it contains the tools you need to accelerate growth, innovate your way to the forefront of the market, and put yourself on the fast-track to success today. Simply read on to find out how you can do the same *FASTER* – and how a few simple shifts in strategy, thinking, and the way you're both presenting and packaging your products, services, and solutions (or even your personal brand) can help you quickly vault right over any obstacle standing in your way.

>>*FASTFORWARDING:*
SIMPLE WAYS TO THINK F.A.S.T.E.R.

Case Study: Coca-Cola – When young adults in Australia stopped drinking Coca-Cola's soft drink products as often as they had in the past, and started getting together more often online than in real-life, the company knew needed to radically reinvent its strategy to connect with them both online and off. But rather than take out millions in TV or radio advertising? And rather than try and cook up all sorts of crazy new flavors? Coca-Cola instead printed the 150 most popular Australian boys' and girls' first names on Coke bottles—bottles it was already manufacturing and selling—and via cost-effective social, online, and mobile media programs—invited citizens to share them and strike up conversation. Within 3 months, it had successfully blanketed the nation with its messaging and increased consumption among young adults by double digits. The campaign proved so clever and cost-effective that it later came to the U.S. and other territories in a big way as well.

Case Study: Topgolf – One of the world's most storied and successful games, the sport of golf nonetheless struggles with how to attract younger audiences who are frequently strapped for time, money, and attention. However, firms such as Topgolf have helped reignite widespread interest not by investing in high-tech equipment so much as simply introducing a business model that makes the golfing experience shorter, more social, and more accessible to everyone. In essence, the company is simply helping people get to fun parts of the game sooner. So rather than compete on discount pricing, which players can get addicted to, and erode its business's returns and perceived value over time? Topgolf instead offers premium entertainment experiences so engaging that players can't stop talking about them – and gives golfers the freedom to decide exactly how they want to experience the game, plus access to a slew other conveniently-located on-site attractions. Just by reimagining its facilities as one-stop family entertainment centers, Topgolf is finding massive success by putting a fresh spin on a formula that country clubs once pioneered.

Case Study: The New Library – In recent years, local libraries have struggled to attract new visitors. Happily, many are enjoying a new lease on life today just by rethinking the role that they can play in their community. For example, a ways back, one facility in the Dutch town of Almere was tanking – attendance was down, memberships were plummeting, and residents complained that the place was too dull and boring. Happily, all staff had to do to reverse the trend was survey members to find out what would interest them, and borrow a page from the hospitality business to help reinvent the branch. Removing piles of untouched stacks, library leaders instead reclaimed underused space in the building and repurposed it as a café; restaurant; coworking center; video gaming facility; and event space at which local artists and musicians were invited to perform. Within months, the facility went from struggling to breaking all-time performance records.

Case Study: Liberty Mutual Insurance – Liberty Mutual was looking to find ways to reduce accidents, minimize customer costs, and find ways to get drivers to behave more safely behind the wheel. Amazingly for a business operating in such a highly-regulated and -competitive field, one of its most popular solutions wasn't to roll out a worldwide educational initiative, training program, or public awareness campaign. Rather, it was to create and launch a downloadable app called *Highway Hero* for smartphones that lets you turn driving into a game. In effect, the better you behave on the road, not only the more points that you can score, but the better the real-world insurance policy discount you can win.

Case Study: SPiN Ping Pong – Ping pong originated as an after-dinner diversion for aristocrats in Victorian-era England. Today, it's also become one of the most popular evening choices for Millennials in big cities such as Washington DC and New York thanks to the efforts of SPiN – a high-energy chain of venues where you can enjoy craft cocktails, fine dining, and Saturday-night DJ sets without ever having to pick up a ball. Players can jump right into the game, which you pay for by the hour, and stop anytime they want to socialize, without ever having to clean up, because someone is always sweeping up the floor and dumping balls back into your bucket.

->DISRUPTING YOURSELF:

**TAKING A MORE FORWARD-THINKING
APPROACH TO LEADERSHIP**

I. HOW TO LEAD IN THE AGE OF CHANGE

So much for the idea of "status quo." While modern executives are no strangers to change and disruption, it bears reminding that things only get more topsy-turvy for working professionals from here. In fact, according to recent surveys by researchers at today's top management consulting firms, no two days on the job will ever be the same again. That's because across every region of the world, and every commercial sector, market leaders explain that the only consistent theme you can count on in coming years is unpredictability.

Think you've got a handle on how fast today's business world moves? Think again. As we ourselves were shocked to find while researching recent book *Lead with Your Heart*, uncertainty is now the only certain at work; the next 10 years will bring more change than the prior 10,000; and – thanks to rapid advancements in technology and communications tools – the one thing organizational leaders can count on going forward is that they'll only be hit with more unforeseen disruptions harder, faster, and from more angles than ever before. So what's a forward-thinking executive to do if they want to help their enterprise stay ahead of the curve? Simple: Apply a simple accelerant, and learn to think faster, by changing up their leadership and management style to make leadership a concept that scales. In effect, by providing workers the insights that they need to make smarter decisions on the fly, and equipping staffers will all the tools that they need to stay better attuned to the now near-constant signals that the marketplace is sending them, it's possible to become much faster about addressing and adapting to these emerging developments in turn.

Bearing this in mind, and that business and cultural trends are now evolving at an unprecedented pace, it's no surprise that business leaders around the world note that strategic priorities for any organization hoping to get ahead in coming years must also evolve. Among the concepts they say it's now vital to champion to your staff if you want to think and move faster as an enterprise are the need to:

- Develop and maximize a globally-aware and -influenced pool of talent
- Foster a culture of employee engagement and continuous learning
- Put productivity, not process, at the heart of your operating strategy
- Dare to consistently disrupt your operations before outside forces disrupt them for you
- Make a commitment to ongoing organizational improvement

But most importantly, they also note that the best way to get ahead in uncertain times is to always be doubling down and reinvesting in your people – and that doing so can pay off in huge ways, because people are your most important asset today.

***

>> >> THE BEST WAY TO GET AHEAD IN UNCERTAIN TIMES IS TO ALWAYS DOUBLE DOWN AND REINVEST IN YOUR PEOPLE >> >>

***

Taking this into account, today's most effective leaders realize that here and now – while things are going well, and you can most afford to take chances – is the most opportune time to teach your organization to move faster by starting to make a host of smart investments in initiatives that drive constant learning and growth for their organization. And that it's also the best time to start encouraging staffers to get behind the idea of making more insight-driven decisions, and educating themselves through a running process of trial and error that involves constantly brainstorming and testing a variety of new strategies and solutions.

Because in uncertain times, as we discovered by speaking with hundreds of market leaders, the irony is that you've got to take *more* risks, not fewer if you want to get ahead. However, these risks have to come in the form of small, smart, cost-effective bets designed as ongoing learning experiments that can help you quickly gain deeper insights into the shape of changing operating landscapes and make better and more informed choices as you become more knowledgeable. Likewise, to stay relevant – let alone ahead of the curve – organizations also have to start being more deliberate about putting systems and programs in place that can help frontline staffers quickly surface great ideas (whether suggested by customers, partners, or colleagues) and take on more of an ownership role in helping drive workplace decisions. Again, if you want to think and move faster, you've got to streamline your organizational structure to act as a springboard for growth – and remove the day-to-day roadblocks that often get in staffers' way.

That's because, ironically, studies of the world's most innovative firms repeatedly show that end-users – everyday customers, strategic partners, the various internal/external stakeholders that we serve, etc. – are the #1 best, most reliable proven source where organizations get successful new ideas. Given that findings also show that most of these ideas can be implemented in 30 days or less to boot, it also demonstrates that if you want to think and move faster as an enterprise, you need to stay well-attuned and responsive to these incoming signals as well. And yet, at the same time, research also tells us that less than a third of organizations have effective systems in place for capturing this feedback and using it to create winning solutions. Keeping this in mind, the real question you should be asking yourself as an executive leader going forward – and encouraging your coworkers to ask themselves – isn't "do we have what it takes to compete" at your organization. It's "are you doing everything you can to give your people all the tools and resources that they need to be listening to the signals the marketplace is constantly sending you, and promptly and intelligently responding to them in turn?"

For example, Dell EMC is a market leader in the field of IT and big data. It has over 60,000 employees worldwide. But when it has a huge, hard problem it just can't seem to solve? It applies the *FASTER* model to accelerate problem-solving, and routinely puts the challenge to its employees in the form of an Innovation Contest. In effect, to quickly and cost-efficiently scale its ability to come up with winning business ventures, the company puts up a website where workers are invited to suggest ideas for innovative new solutions – and can comment on these ideas, give colleagues feedback, and vote on which of these concepts are turned into real-world prototypes and products. Ironically though, it turns out that many of the firm's most successful ventures are happening when employees worldwide are independently teaming up on their own time to bring new ideas that they found online to life – many of which weren't technically contest winners.

Likewise, you can see a host of government agencies doing a similar end-run around traditional bureaucratic and budgeting hurdles, and employing like-minded solutions for accelerating and scaling innovation, at Challenge.gov – a website where institutions like the Centers for Disease Control and Prevention and U.S. Army put up contests asking the general public and members of the private sector for help with tasks like designing better healthcare programs or building better underground bunkers. Prizes for winning solutions can often exceed $1 million – but it's often a small price to pay by these organizations, comparatively, for creating platforms that allow these agencies to radically multiply the number of winning ideas, insights, and solutions that they're able to surface.

Long story short? When it comes to getting ahead despite disruption, and finding ways to successfully navigate through change, even as an experienced team leader, it often pays to find more ways to step back and let others take the lead. The more you look to make leadership and innovation concepts that scale, and put programs and platforms in place to rapidly transform ideas into reality – say a running series of 48-hour hackathon events (in which participants must create working product prototypes in less than two days), or a six-week company-wide design contest that crowdsources concepts for new business opportunities to explore? The faster you'll be able to think and move, and more successful you'll be, no matter what the future brings.

II. HOW TO MAKE BETTER BUSINESS DECISIONS

Recently, I was invited by one of America's top military leaders to share my thoughts on how to make leadership a principle that was ingrained at every level throughout an organization, and make smarter decisions in an era of constant change. My answer was simple: Learn to think faster by emboldening and empowering staffers to take action more frequently by giving them more opportunities to speak up and assume leadership roles – and put platforms in place that allow them to more rapidly ingest internal/external insights, deploy complementing ideas, and adapt these ideas to be more successful in turn based on feedback they gain from these efforts. That said, getting workers to embrace the idea of *intrapreneurial* thinking – i.e. taking more ownership of various programs, and operating like entrepreneurs, or internal change agents – isn't a process that happens overnight. Which begs the question: How can you promote similar shifts in thinking among your organization, especially if the idea of change doesn't come easily to it?

A few concepts that I'd argue it's important to teach your people here are as follows:

• Innovation isn't always about cutting-edge breakthroughs or game-changing technologies, as the *FASTER* formula illustrates. Noting this, it pays to remind staff at every turn that simple shifts in business strategy or operating models can be every bit as powerful at driving huge wins for your organization as new technology and groundbreaking scientific discoveries. In fact, as research shows, innovation can simply be a matter of perspective—and process of constant reinvention. And enterprises of every size and background have the ability to leverage its core principles to succeed more frequently going forward. For example, one Fortune 500 we work with has found ways to fast-track internal learning and growth by holding regular breakfast meetings and educational salons where senior leaders and junior hires are encouraged to sit down, share insights, and collaborate in casual settings. Likewise, a government institution we've partnered with is using virtual reality and online gaming installations to help training programs better connect and resonate with younger, more tech-savvy recruits.

• What's more, as noted, surveys repeatedly tell us that end-users for our services and solutions are the single best source where organizations get successful and innovative new ideas. Likewise, frontline workers – i.e. salespeople and customer reps, who are often closest to these information sources – are often the most informed audience inside any given institution. Taking this into account, it's important to put platforms and programs in place at every turn that allow these individuals to surface breaking insights and trends, and let great ideas bubble up from the bottom, not just flow on down from an executive team at the top. From consumer giants like Starbucks and Elmer's Products to government organizations like the National Institutes of Health and U.S. Dept. of Defense, more and more firms are turning to the concept of *open innovation* – inviting feedback and contribution of ideas and input from outside sources, including private/public institutions and general citizens – as a means of scaling and accelerating innovation. In effect, they're realizing that the more radically you can multiply the number of resources and insights available to you, the more radically you can multiply the speed at which you can solve any given challenge.

• Likewise, in addition to providing staffers with more opportunities to try new things going forward, and promoting the idea of grand-scale thought leadership, I'd argue that it's also important to champion concepts like rapid deployment and learning amongst your workforce as well. After all, the more feedback from any given operating landscape that you can get, and the faster you can get it, the more rapidly you can use this information to improve your business programs and strategies, and the better off your organization will be. In essence, flexibility and agility are the essence of future-proofing, and the ability to learn rapidly, and quickly translate those learnings into actionable business strategy, is the ultimate source of competitive advantage. Worth noting: Most organizations can go from conceptualizing new products, services, and solutions to launching them in less than 90 days (noting that less than 30 days is the current gold standard), and many run regular events and contests – e.g. *Shark Tank-style* competitions for surfacing entrepreneurial ideas – that invite contributors to invent working prototypes in a matter of days.

• It's also important to teach your people that the idea that a plan or program has to be 100% perfect and flawless – because it stops us from moving forward – is often the enemy of "finished" and "done." And that the idea of working on projects until they're "good enough" – because it forces us to hone our time and efforts, work to fixed deadlines, and allows us to quickly gain that real-world feedback faster that we need to help shape ideas for the better – is often the start of something great. The more you can get people to adopt a *minimum viable product (MVP)* mindset, where they routinely use the least time and resources possible to create working concepts, then roll out their solutions and learn from these concepts' deployment, the better off you'll be.

In effect, the more you ingrain these principles – and work to both create leaders at every level and implement an innovation model that incorporates a running series of smart, cost-effective learning and experimentation programs throughout its framework – the more effective your enterprise will be. As today's most successful leaders are aware, change is far less difficult to deal with when you make a point to think *FASTER*, promote positive disruption within your organization, and constantly stay in tune with changing times and trends by regularly changing up your solutions and operating strategies as well.

III. HOW TO DEAL WITH DISRUPTION

Succeeding in hugely disruptive environments isn't about avoiding risks. As those accomplished in the art of getting ahead *FASTER* know, it's actually about taking more risks—albeit calculated and controlled ones. If you study leading innovators, you'll notice something interesting: They never stop innovating, and are always exploring an array of new business strategies and ventures. That's because staying ahead of the curve and making smarter decisions in disruptive environments is largely a process of controlled speculation: Being *risk-averse*, not *risk-free*.

Essentially, market leaders actively manage innovation the same way you would manage a financial portfolio. Diversify. Monitor. Consistently readjust. This means placing multiple bets. Some of these gambles will be high risk, high reward. Some will be low risk, low return. Not all will pay off. But by pursuing all, you help grow your organization's learning and capabilities, and gain deeper insights into changing markets.

Consider that Starbucks is the world's largest chain of coffee houses. It famously describes itself as "in the people biz serving coffee, not the coffee biz serving people." The company would be crazy to upset its customers, right? But it constantly puts its Arabica beans on the line. Starbucks is routinely rolling out new business strategies and programs, such as new store concepts, products, and payment options, even before most of these concepts are finished and error-free. Why? Because it understands the power of moving FASTER, and says it would rather be first than flawless, make mistakes than miss an opportunity, and fall flat than fail to be swifter to establish market beachheads than rivals. And it makes a point to train its people in a simple, but hugely powerful principle that sets the business up to succeed time and again: In the face of ongoing change and disruption, the only thing to truly be afraid of is not changing as well.

IDENTIFYING TOMORROW'S LEADERS

Tomorrow's leaders will possess only two defining characteristics: The ability to solve problems and create results. Accordingly, it's vital to instill more bootstrapping values (for example, a culture of ownership, entrepreneurship, and accountability) in employees, and teach them how to more effectively think dynamically and olve problems in context.

Case in point: At Intuit, a personal finance software maker, senior management says its sole role now is "to remove the speed bumps in experimenters' way." To this extent, its employees are routinely encouraged to think like business owners and experiment like mad scientists, bringing new products and projects to market as fast as possible, learning from these efforts, and sharing their insights with the broader organization at large.

Workers are then encouraged to come up with still more new ideas, and use online collaboration tools to secure resources, support, and insights from peers. They then go to market with real-world prototypes as fast as possible. Intuit's employees can now do this without getting the management or legal team's approval (yet more speed bumps removed), and dozens of revenue-generating products and features have resulted.

SKILLS FOR THE FUTURE

The capabilities and tools needed to succeed in business today and tomorrow look very different from those that were needed to succeed yesterday. Below are the skills you should be teaching employees in a world where systems routinely break down, variables are constantly changing, and uncertainty is the only certain.

- **Make smarter decisions.** Time, effort, and energy are finite resources, meaning that every decision comes with two costs: Opportunity, as well as financial. Teach employees how to factor both in when making decisions and considering which ventures to pursue. The more they consider where efforts are best focused from a long-term perspective, the more successful they'll be.

- **Manage time.** Common wisdom says that "busy is good." But truthfully, it's only good if you're spending this time steadily working toward achieving your stated goals. When deciding where to focus, teach employees to concentrate on accomplishing tasks that directly move them further toward achieving your organization's overarching objectives, and avoid becoming distracted by busywork or lower-priority demands that often cause us to lose focus on the big picture.

- **Maximize effort.** Successful leaders always find ways to win in every scenario besides pure profits. That way, they're always able to benefit from any given choice, and use what they've gained from the undertaking as a springboard to fuel continued growth and advancement. For example, by taking on a new project or client that helps you push your company's capabilities in new directions, you may gain invaluable new connections, insights, and experience into promising new avenues of growth or opportunity.

- **Focus on long-term goals.** Rather than simply concentrate on the here and now, train workers today to also be purposefully seeking out the tools, talents, and resources they'll need to succeed tomorrow. Perhaps transitioning a lower-ranking or lower-paying job role isn't such a bad idea if it gets them invaluable training and experience into emerging areas that will be in demand in the future. Likewise, maybe spending less time trying to sell more existing products and focusing on successfully launching innovative new ones is a better investment in your organization's growth capabilities as well.

- **Think fluidly.** Leaders need to learn to make firm business decisions despite uncertainty. The simplest way to do so is to exercise "strong, but weakly held opinions." Teach leaders to do their homework up front and gather as much business intelligence as possible, then act. And, after assessing the results of their choices, they should adjust their approaches to be more successful based on the insights gained from these efforts.

• **Embrace failure.** Modern successes consistently experiment with new business strategies and solutions, and aren't afraid to fail. Think of failure as the price of getting an education—a price that you can control. It's alright to fail as long as you're failing quickly and cost-effectively, and learning from mistakes and using the insights gained to improve future tries.

• **Future-proof.** To keep themselves, and your business, ahead of the curve, teach employees to prioritize ongoing education and professional development. Train them to regularly stop and ask themselves: What types of talents, training, and educational experiences will be in demand tomorrow? Then have them purposefully seek out the opportunities they'll need to get these assets right here, right now today. That way, both your organization and its workforce will be ready to greet the future long before it comes knocking.

• **Fix problems.** If your organization finds itself dealing with the same issues over and over, there's probably a larger underlying issue that keeps causing them. Encourage workers to purposefully seek these challenges out, and to stop curing symptoms and start solving problems. Instead of struggling with side effects, you will all find that it's better to fix what ails you once and be done with it.

The biggest challenges we face when it comes to getting ahead faster in business are, ironically, the same ones we often face in everyday life: Teaching ourselves and our colleagues to be more open to change, and more flexible and diligent about responding to it. So instead of fighting change, teach employees to prepare themselves to greet it more effectively, and be more amenable to rolling with the punches.

Be bold. Be creative. Be open to new perspectives. And be willing to take some smart risks. The more you can teach this formula, the more you'll give employees all the tools they need to stay in tune with changing times and trends, stay on top of their field, and stay ahead of the curve as well.

CHARACTERISTICS OF FUTURE-PROOF LEADERS

Today's business leaders must remain focused on what's next. Here is a list of attributes those best equipped to move *FASTER* should embody.

• Crave curiosity. As a forward-thinking executive, it is more important to ask "why?" than "what?" so that we can dive into the root cause of an issue and understand the value shifts driving today's trends.

• Act courageously. As humans we are wired to reject change, and the future is synonymous with change. A good futurist must recognize that the insights we share will make others feel uncomfortable, but it is in that discomfort that growth occurs.

• Think outrageously. The ability to think provocatively is paramount to being able to see ahead of the curve, and react faster. To expand our thinking (and that of our leadership and stakeholders), we must stretch our minds beyond our comfort zone.

• Connect the dots. It is not enough to collect the dots (or trends). A forward-looking executive also must connect them to uncover patterns. To understand what's next, we must analyze the intersection of trends and make sense of the patterns they form.

• Think in multiples. As good futurists, we must be able to think in simultaneous, multiple futures rather than the traditional, single, linear forecast. Being able to consider myriad paths beyond the official future allows us to create robust and resilient strategies that will be successful no matter which future emerges.

IV. WHY IT PAYS TO INVEST IN TOMORROW'S LEADERS

From the consumer products and electronics sectors to technology and retail businesses, the world's most innovative industries also consistently rank among its most-forward thinking fields. But even for market leaders that may find themselves operating in sectors like these (which are renowned for going from strength to strength by practicing core principles of disruption, and routinely reinventing themselves to remain relevant), it bears reminding. Continued growth won't just come from ongoing research and development into breakthrough technologies. It will also come from making investments in another area in which innovative businesses tend to excel: Specifically, cultivating world-class talent, and making it an ongoing priority to create leaders at every level.

But why is investing in human capital key to sustaining growth – and moving much faster going forward? The answers lie in strategic thinking and planning for tomorrow. As surveys of hundreds of the world's most innovative companies show, having more time, money, or manpower is no longer the secret to getting ahead in business, or creating competitive advantage. Instead, the world's most accomplished organizations stay ahead of the curve by working to encourage disruptive thinking in hires – and constantly giving their people more opportunities to share their insights and experiment with creative new solutions. (In other words, in the face of changing environments, they constantly strive to cultivate entrepreneurial thinking in workers, listen more closely to target audiences, and find better ways to tap into the power of their people to find ways to smartly adapt to new market evolutions.)

What's more, finding ways to more actively promote creative thinking and make cultivating a growth mindset a routine way of operating across the board will only become more important for business leaders in every field in coming years as well. Consider that we'll see more technological breakthroughs in the next 10 years than prior civilizations did in centuries – and that the big theme coming into the next decade is *unpredictability*. According to business leaders, uncertainty is now the only certain, and confidence in enterprises' ability to achieve both short- and medium-term growth is at an all-time record low. Great talent is also still hard to come by, studies show, and there's a huge shortage of workers who possess the skills needed to translate the mountain of data we're all gathering these days into actionable business results. Even more eye-opening, despite investing billions in digital upskilling, business executives across the globe say that they're still struggling to get key info they need to make intelligent choices in today's fast-moving world. Simultaneously, we're all being forced to adapt to exponential new advancements from blockchain technologies to artificial intelligence and virtual reality solutions – all of which are hitting us harder, faster, and from more angles than ever before.

The net result? In a world that's changing this fast, and has become so unpredictable, odds are that the way things have "always been done" are no longer the best way to do them. And organizations of every size and scope need to be more active about promoting meritocracies when it comes to decision making, and championing cultures of learning and growth, since succeeding is now less about our talents as individual professionals, and more about empowering our collective workforces to make change happen. In essence, right here, right now – while things are going well, and you can most afford to take chances – is the best time to be doubling down and investing in initiatives that drive continuing learning and growth. Likewise, it's also the best time to be encouraging yourselves and your colleagues to embrace the idea of continued learning through constant trial and error – the surest way to succeed in any fast-changing environment.

>> >> IN UNCERTAIN TIMES, YOU'VE GOT TO TAKE MORE RISKS, NOT FEWER, IF YOU WANT TO GET AHEAD IN BUSINESS >> >>

Because in uncertain times, counterintuitively, you've got to take more risks, not fewer if you want to get ahead in business. However, these risks have to come in the form of small, smart, cost-effective bets designed as ongoing learning experiments that can help you quickly gain deeper insights into the shape of changing customer needs and markets and make better and more informed choices as you get smarter. Likewise, you've also got to start being more deliberate about putting systems and solutions in place that can help frontline employees more effectively stay attuned and responsive to shifting cultural or market landscapes. Risky is the new safe, so to speak – and you've got to make a point to prepare both your organization, and your people, to start taking more risks going forward.

Happily, a growing number of today's most in-demand industries have cultivated a long, proud history of putting innovation first, and partnering with organizations and entities in other fields. (Noting that the more that they encourage collaboration, the more resources and capabilities that they can bring to bear to solve any given challenge.) And the results speak for themselves, helping vault these industries to become global powerhouses in the areas of growth and innovation. Maintaining this leadership role clearly remains a continued priority for executives in these fields. But to achieve this goal, enterprises will not only need to keep doing what they're doing in terms of raising the high-tech bar. They'll also have to make an ongoing point to invest in tomorrow's leaders, and give them all the tools, support, and runway they need to keep delivering tomorrow's most game-changing advancements.

V. WHY EMOTIONAL INTELLIGENCE IS CRUCIAL TO EFFECTIVE LEADERSHIP

If you're wondering how to build better relationships at work, and more effectively motivate colleagues to think faster, start by considering how emotional intelligence (EQ) affects leadership – and how to go about boosting yours. But just what is emotional intelligence, and why is it an increasingly important topic for modern professionals to consider? The answers may surprise you.

According to industry experts, emotional intelligence (EQ) describes one's ability to identify and manage their own emotions, as well as empathize with and manage others' emotions as well. Put simply, it defines your capacity to understand and express your feelings, as well as comprehend what motivates others and how to successfully collaborate with them. Noting this, and that five generations are now colliding in the workplace, each of which boasts its own distinctive goals and communications styles, it's more imperative than ever for modern leaders to be empathetic. Given that the World Economic Forum notes that nine in ten top performers boast greater emotional intelligence than peers, and the universally growing importance of emotional intelligence training for leaders, the concept should be at the top of your list to master.

Wondering why EQ is an essential trait to prioritize for any executive going forward? For starters, as Daniel Goleman, author of Building Blocks of Emotional Intelligence explains, EQ is a far greater predictor of success than professional ability or inborn talent. In fact, as he states, a person can be highly intelligent and boast considerable technical aptitude, but unless they possess high levels of emotional intelligence, they'll have trouble discovering how to build successful relationships at work and never become a great leader. Moreover, EQ is a complex trait, whose attributes are split along a broad spectrum that breaks down into four individual categories that executives looking to build positive working relationships must seek to master: Self-awareness; self-management; social awareness; and relationship management.

Self-awareness is the basic building block of emotional intelligence, speaking to your ability to understand your emotions, as well as the potential impact they may have on your on-the-job performance and professional relationships. Self-management instead defines your ability to maintain self-control under duress, to manage personal behavior and responsibilities, and capacity to adapt when faced with adverse circumstances. Social awareness denotes one's ability to effectively read other people's moods, and gauge their needs and concerns. Lastly, relationship management speak to your potential to lead, inspire, and influence others, not to mention successfully build relationships at work and manage conflict and change in life and business.

In effect, an emotionally intelligent organization is one that sports positive and productive workplace where colleagues trust one another, freely collaborate, and feel comfortable speaking up, sharing their thoughts, and taking action. Similarly, an emotionally intelligent leader is an individual whom colleagues feel can relate to them and that is able to motivate teams and individuals, skillfully resolve conflict, and inspire others to take positive action. Bearing this in mind, the greater EQ that you possess as a leader, the greater potential that you'll have to successfully bring groups of individuals and disparate business divisions together to accomplish shared tasks and solve hard problems in short order. Likewise, the more emotional intelligence that you can bring to bear when dealing with clients, the better attuned you will be to customers' needs and concerns, and greater capacity you'll have to come up with winning business solutions.

Striving to boost emotional intelligence isn't just good for workplace productivity, performance, and morale – and a good way to build more positive working relationships – either. It's also good for career advancement as well. As far back as a decade ago, 71% of employers were already indicating that they preferred individuals with high emotional intelligence over high IQ when weighing prospective hires, making EQ a crucial talent to possess for job seekers – especially prospective leaders. Likewise, when Google founders Sergey Brin and Larry Page researched the professional capabilities that set top performers apart from peers, they discovered that soft skills like EQ were a better predictor of success than technical know-how. Noting this, it's no surprise that more and more leadership positions in today's market aren't going to those with better academic pedigrees and training. Rather, they're going to those working professionals who boast higher EQ, a more advanced background in emotional intelligence training, and superior communications and teamwork abilities.

After all, to achieve lofty goals, and solve complex challenges, we typically need to build strong relationships at work, align ourselves with like-minded individuals, and draw upon an assortment of colleagues' skills and talents. Leaders who possess strong emotional intelligence not only have the potential to build stronger relationships, and assemble more effective teams. They also enjoy greater ability to motivate contributors to excel, and successfully complete tasks, especially those that require businesses to leverage or mix-and-match the abilities of individuals with different skill sets and backgrounds. In essence, the higher your management team's EQ, the more creative and innovative your organization will become. Likewise, adding even just a single point of EQ to its capabilities can help you 10X your business' performance, making finding more effective ways to ingrain emotional intelligence training in leaders a topic that every enterprise should be exploring. Bottom line? The more you make a point to prioritize emotional intelligence as a leader, the faster you'll be able to move – and more successful both you and your business will be.

VI. 7 SKILLS YOU SHOULD BE TEACHING EMPLOYEES

The world of business continues to evolve at an unprecedented pace, with half of all S&P 500 companies expected to be replaced within the next decade. Moreover, the first place that organizations need to adapt if they want to survive lies in the area of evolving workplace skills and upskilling their workforce, according to HR People + Strategy. Clearly, those talents which bring enterprises success in tomorrow's working world will be greatly different than those which have served them in the past. Following, you'll find seven new skills that every business should be adding to its employee learning and development plan if it wants to think *FASTER*, and succeed in an age of constant change. And for that matter, the benefits of upskilling employees in this manner, as well as why it pays to be making this retraining a priority.

Creativity – Shh, don't tell: Innovation is just another word for *improvisation*. Likewise, it's often a matter of perspective, as simple shifts in business or communications strategy can prove every bit as powerful as game-changing breakthroughs at driving positive results for your organization. Don't have the time or cash to think 3-5 years ahead into the future, or invest heavily in giving your business plan a huge overhaul? No worries: You can succeed by teaching employees to *think differently* here and now instead. Train them to ask themselves questions like: What other possible uses for our products and services exist? How can we repackage or represent existing solutions to better appeal to new audiences? Are there ways we could be doing in a single step what's currently taking us several? You may be surprised at just how quickly simple exercises such as these can send profits soaring.

Communications – Wondering how to most effectively train employees to be leaders? Take a tip from one of the world's largest technology firms, who once created a scientific method to analyze nearly every HR- and job-related decision that the company had made in order to see what made its top-performing employees so successful. Surprisingly, what they discovered was that technical skills such as an individual's ability to manipulate software and create cutting-edge applications weren't what gave these executives an edge. Rather, it was soft skills such as the ability to effectively communicate with coworkers and empathize with others that were likelier to determine who would be an effective leader in the end. Especially worth noting if you're an employer: STEM (science, technology, engineering, and math) capabilities ranked among the least important determinants of success to be found amongst top employees – high emotional intelligence (EQ) proved a better predictor of superior on-the-job performance instead. Keeping this in mind, training workers to be strong communicators is every bit as crucial to finding success in tomorrow's working world as training them in today's most cutting-edge software engineering techniques or management theories.

***

>> >> TRAINING WORKERS TO BE BETTER COMMUNICATORS IS EVERY BIT AS CRUCIAL AS TEACHING THEM TODAY'S MOST CUTTING-EDGE TECHNICAL SKILLS >> >>

***

Multi-Tasking – According to researchers at IBM, constant change is the new normal in the workplace, and unpredictability the only thing we can predict. Noting this, colleagues' efforts will only be further stretched between more tasks and projects in coming years, and their attention split increasingly thin. As a result, teaching workers how to effectively juggle a multitude of responsibilities and deadlines will become a growingly important topic to address in employee learning and development plans going forward. Given that they'll continue to be pulled in multiple directions in coming years, and with greater frequency, it's vital that you train associates to effectively manage multiple tasks, and perform work efficiently. Likewise, you'll also want to teach them how to better relieve stress, and the importance of maintaining a healthy work-life balance.

Agility – As noted earlier, numerous businesses can now go from conceptualizing to executing upon a new idea in under 90 days, a process which can also take under 30 days for many firms. That's because these organizations understand that the quicker you can deploy a new idea, the faster you can get feedback from the marketplace – and more rapidly you can use these insights to enhance business strategy. That's why it's vital to also teach employees the importance of adopting a minimum viable product (MVP) mindset, wherein they use the least time and resources possible to create and test working prototypes. The faster you can bring concepts to life (and determine how audiences react to them in real-world environments), and more rapidly you can translate these learnings into action, the more successful you'll be.

Listening – Want to rapidly create positive change in your organization, and consistently find ways to stay ahead of the curve? Train your team to grow bigger ears. Unfortunately, nearly half of all businesses aren't even surveying or polling clients, let alone collecting actionable information from customer service reps, salespeople, and other frontline leaders. Bearing this in mind, teach your people to keep their antennae peeled for incoming signals from the marketplace at every turn. The better you become at hearing them, the better off your business will be.

Empathy – Of course, it's also important to train workers to be more empathetic if you want them to stay better attuned to any operating environment and respond rapidly and productively to changes within it. That's because doing so frequently requires us to relate to the needs of customers of coworkers; engage with these individuals; and find ways to inspire them to take positive action at every turn. Similarly, boasting strong emotional intelligence is also key to leading people and helping guide them past setbacks, and through times of great uncertainty and upheaval. So if you want workers to be successful leaders, teach them to be more empathetic – it'll make them more open-minded, flexible, and resilient in the end.

Leadership – Trade secret: In a world of new and novel problems, it also pays to teach your people to be capable of applying both logic and creativity to solving any given challenge. What's more, in increasingly uncertain business environments, it's vital to train them to make firm decisions even in the absence of perfect information as well. This can be done by introducing them to the concept of *strong, but weakly-held opinions* – wherein you do your homework and make the best choice given current insights, but remain open to revising action plans as more feedback is gained. Likewise, it's also important to underscore the importance of keeping a cool head under duress, and acting thoughtfully, even amidst ongoing disruption. While leaders can't predict every twist or turn the marketplace will take, they always have the ability to pivot their strategies to better steer organizations towards success – and the ability to course-correct and revise those plans further as scenarios continue to develop.

VII. HOW TO SHOW EMPLOYEES THAT THEY'RE YOUR GREATEST ASSET

Surprise – as surveys of hundreds of the world's most innovative companies show, having more time, money, or manpower isn't the secret to getting ahead in business, or creating competitive advantage. Instead, as we found while researching bestselling book *Make Change Work for You*, the world's most accomplished organizations strive to create leaders at every level, and constantly give people more opportunities to speak up, share their insights, and experiment with creative new solutions. (In other words, as discussed earlier, they constantly strive to cultivate entrepreneurial thinking in workers, listen more closely to customers, and find better ways to tap into the power of their people.) But with employee *incentivization* every bit as important to driving forward growth and momentum as innovation, what's the best way to let colleagues know that their work is valued – and that they're number one in your book? And with so many great employee appreciation and recognition ideas to potentially draw upon when doing so, how can you determine which will most resonate with them? Here are five ways you can get workers excited and engaged, and transform every individual at your business into a potential change agent.

***

>> >> *SOMETIMES, THE SIMPLEST EMPLOYEE RECOGNITION IDEAS ARE THE BEST*>> >>

***

Create Opportunities to Contribute – Sometimes, the simplest employee recognition ideas are the best. For example, when one global healthcare leader wants to discover big, game-changing ideas to pursue? It creates online forums where participants are invited to share ideas, source feedback and support from colleagues, and vote which concepts should be turned into real-world solutions. Similarly, when one of the industry's largest global finance firms is looking to identify prospective candidates for promotion to leadership roles, even though they may be young and inexperienced on paper, or not have a background managing people? It holds regular competitions in which employees from every department are invited to collaborate in small teams to come up with working product prototypes in the course of a single weekend. Still more clients hold regular dinners where senior leaders provide time to sit down and swap ideas with new hires; provide ongoing conferences, workshops, and strategic retreats where colleagues spend time sharing ideas and learning from other; and purposefully put employees through a rotation of job roles to help them gain new insights, connections, and skills. All of these employee recognition ideas help reinforce an important point: *Our company is listening to what you have to say, and every employee's contributions matter.* This kind of recognition can be even more powerful than financial incentives when it comes to promoting an organizational culture of greatness.

Offer Unique Upsides and Benefits – If you want to create more compelling job offers, and attract and retain top performers by keeping your employees happier, it helps to analyze your ideal hires' needs and customize benefits to each prospective candidate. For example, one major quick-service restaurant chain not only provides health insurance for employees who work 25 or more hours weekly to reward an older audience of part-time workers looking to supplement their retirement income. It also provides college tuition for many candidates, because an equally large segment of employees are college-bound individuals and twenty-somethings. Many leaders in other fields are also following suit, and shifting away from demanding that employees be chained to a desk during daytime hours to operating models which emphasize teleworking opportunities and flexible schedules to help attract and keep spirits high amongst workers, especially Millennials, Gen Xers, and Baby Boomers who may be working parents. Customizing the benefits of being a part of your organization can be one of today's most effective employee appreciation ideas, and produce big wins when it comes to boosting worker satisfaction and morale.

Request Regular Creative Input – Crowdsourcing creative contributions from your employees – e.g. inviting them to submit ideas and input en masse – can also be a powerful way for your organization to fast-track growth, and reinforce your appreciation for their skills. Whether asking workers to send you their best designs for new logos; inviting them to film videos for possible consideration in online advertisements; or requesting that they share their best stories for inclusion in eBooks, whitepapers, and brochures, many engaging and dynamic ways exist to get your workforce involved. From photos to podcasts, slideshows to social network posts, these types of user-generated content programs can provide ready opportunities to spotlight key contributors, and put a more human face on your brand as well. Not only do these types of programs feel more authentic and genuine for the effort. They also provide added chances to uncover winning solutions more rapidly, and shine the spotlight where it's rightfully deserved – on the everyday employees who make your business the wonderful place to work it is – as well.

Promote Professional Growth and Development – Ongoing learning and growth is the basic building block of a successful business, and a successful career, today. So make a specific point to also help employees pick up in-demand training, experience, and skills wherever possible as well. (Among the best employee appreciation ideas you can implement.) Sometimes, this means setting budgets aside to invest in formal education, training, or certification programs. But just as often, it can include simply providing workers with the access and time that they need to sit down with colleagues from different departments to discuss best practices, or to gain deeper insight into new areas of the business, new technologies, and new growth markets. If you're looking to start simple, remember: Efforts here can be as simple as springing for a pizza night that brings the marketing and software development teams together to learn more about how each other works, and share ideas for improvement. The key is to actively connect workers with resources and opportunities that can help them learn, grow, and expand their skill set, and become more valuable on the job.

Help Colleagues Shine – Most of tomorrow's workforce – regardless of age or background – won't measure success in terms of money, but rather their ability to accomplish goals and make a difference in their organization or community. They'll also want to work for innovative companies, and expect to run their own forward-thinking entrepreneurial ventures at some point. If you're hoping to boost spirits, and employee engagement, it helps to remember that you can do so by providing clear goals, an engaging variety of assignments to tackle, and cultivating a go-getting attitude in your organization. Likewise, you'll further want to provide more mentorship and ongoing feedback in the workplace, as well as more transparency, guidance, and honest input about how the organization is evolving – and how they can personally contribute in ways that make a meaningful difference. And remember, it's common these days for high-performing employees come and go, as they seek to expand their horizons and take on new challenges and roles. If they choose to move on, stay supportive. Not only will doing so reinforce to others that you truly care about them. These selfsame individuals may very well may rejoin your team at a later date more experienced and capable for having done so.

VIII. HOW TO COMMUNICATE WITH EVERY GENERATION

Take a second to stop, pause, and look around you the next time you're at a meeting or event, and you may notice something surprising: The faces of tomorrow's leaders are quickly changing. With 74.5 million members and counting, Millennials, or Gen Yers (individuals roughly 19-35 years of age) are now the single largest generation in America, both in and out of the workplace. What's more, the way in which they communicate, interact, and process information is vastly different than any generation that's come before. In addition, Gen Zers (the generation which follows, members of which were born after 1995) – whose habits and norms vary wildly even from Millennials – are quickly following right behind. Needless to say, as we discovered while putting together recent book *Millennial Marketing: Bridging the Generation Gap*, those of us looking to inspire and motivate these individuals must learn to communicate with them in vastly different ways than with the generations who've come before.

With regard to Generation Y, several important points to note before crafting messages or outreach efforts are as follows. Nowadays, a third of all adults are Millennials. Furthermore, nearly nine in ten don't measure success in terms of money, but rather their ability to accomplish goals and make a difference in their business or community. Roughly 80% want to work for innovative companies, and expect, in fact, to run their own forward-thinking entrepreneurial ventures at some point. In addition, like Boomers, Millennials now hail from a wide swath of age ranges – cultural touchpoints and references that speak to one group of Millennials won't necessarily make sense to all, as you're actually looking at multiple generations rolled into one category.

>> >> *MOST MEMBERS OF GENERATIONS Y AND Z WON'T MEASURE SUCCESS IN TERMS OF MONEY* >> >>

However, it's important to note: Virtually every member of this generation has grown up in an online and connected world, where they're bombarded by media and messaging on a 24/7 daily basis. The net result? Attention spans are shrinking, Millennial audiences are increasingly tuning out messages they don't connect with, and – before they're willing to invest their time and attention in efforts – young professionals increasingly need us to show them how, by getting involved in any given venture, their contributions will make a meaningful difference.

As for Gen Zers, who are following in the footsteps of Millennials, also keep in mind that they're the first generation who've ever grown up in a mobile world, where virtually everything is available on-demand, personalized to taste, and just a click or tap away. Within four years, these individuals will represent nearly a quarter of America's population – and their attention will be harder to capture and hold than ever. Case in point: Gen Zers use five screens a day on average (smartphone, tablet, TV, desktop, and laptop) – as compared to Millennials, who use just three. What's more, Gen Zers are far more social than their forerunners, spending up to 8 hours a day interacting with friends and family – they love opportunities to interact, such as those meeting planners can regularly provide. But when you're attempting to lead or communicate with them, it's also vital to keep in mind that as result of growing up in a wireless world, their average attention span now lasts just eight seconds – less than that of a goldfish. As you can see, providing clear, concise, and engaging messages as part of communications efforts will be key to engaging them. And rest assured, engaging them will indeed be vital to ensuring your organization's future.

Noting these points, as you go about empowering tomorrow's leaders to move faster, and designing programming and outreach efforts that support your endeavors, you'll want to keep the following items in mind:

• Gen Yers and Gen Zers will expect clear goals, an engaging variety of assignments to tackle, and to work for organizations with a go-getting attitude that encourages people to speak up, collaborate, and be more proactive about sharing and acting on ideas.

• These generations will demand greater access to professional training and development programs, as well as more hands-on opportunities to expand their experience and skill sets.

• Going forward, young professionals will seek more mentorship and ongoing feedback in the workplace, and look to you for additional guidance, as the skills in-demand tomorrow will look far different than the ones in-demand today.

• You'll need to educate these natural-born innovators that teamwork and a winning attitude will be key concepts to embrace as projects become more complex, and a growing number of generations and backgrounds collide in the workplace.

• Gen Y and Gen Z will increasingly look to your leadership to provide guidance and ongoing input about what's going on in the organization, as well as ways that they can personally contribute to the cause and make a difference.

A few hints and tips for those hoping to work with these younger generations more effectively going forward are as follows:

• Remember that Millennials and Gen Zers will hail from a wide range of age groups. A Gen Yer could just as easily be a professional starting out on their career journey as a young parent. When crafting communications and outreach efforts, take care to leverage common themes or points of reference that all can recognize – and don't assume that a one-size-fits-all approach will always be most effective.

• Don't market or promote: Tell stories others can empathize with. As researchers are increasingly demonstrating, Millennials aren't responding to routine advertisements or generic messages anymore. Instead, they're looking for causes and efforts that resonate with their values, and that they feel they can connect with and support on a personal level.

• Keep messaging short and to the point, and grab others' attention right from the get-go. To hold Gen Y and Gen Z's interest, it's best to lead with a strong, one-of-a-kind message – and, where appropriate, use vehicles such as humor or heartwarming tales to quickly differentiate. Highly visual, these generations also respond far better to short animations, videos, infographics, charts, and other graphical points of reference than textual elements.

• Make a point to stand out a glance: Gen Y and Gen Zers are used to quickly dismissing the many messages with which they're bombarded. To avoid falling into this trap, help them quickly connect the dots, and explain what makes you and your organization unique, what pain points or problems you can help them solve, and how they can quickly and simply interact with you to create positive outcomes. Give them points of shared interest and incentive to rally behind.

Clearly, Millennials and members of Generation Z look at and interact with the world in far different ways than generations who've come before. But with a few simple shifts in perspective and positioning, it becomes far easier to connect and communicate with them on a meaningful level. Employ the strategies above as you go about crafting your communications efforts, and empowering tomorrow's leaders to succeed, and you'll find it far simpler and more cost-effective to drive interest, fuel ongoing engagement, and get your message heard.

IX. HOW TO SURVIVE & THRIVE DESPITE CONSTANT DISRUPTION

Welcome to 2020 and beyond: A decade of endless high-tech disruption. Blockchain, artificial intelligence, big data, robotics, virtual reality... as a quick look at some of tomorrow's most cutting-edge high-tech trends reveals, the future is suddenly here. Luckily, while continuous change is the new norm in business for executive leaders, four simple shifts in thinking can help you stay ahead of the curve.

MAKE CHANGE YOUR SECRET WEAPON

Trade secret: Innovation is just another word for *improvisation*—and anyone can adapt to new and novel problems the same way leading innovators do... by studying problems, brainstorming original solutions, then steadily trying and improving as they go. For example, when car manufacturer Hyundai was pummeled by a drop in consumer spending during the Great Recession? Unlike competitors, it didn't immediately cut prices or bump up ad spending or promote new product features or incentives. Instead, Hyundai created a program that allowed its salespeople and showroom employees to speak up and share their insights more readily. Hyundai then asked these workers to find out what was going on, and discovered that the reason for spending drops was the risk associated with buying automobiles in uncertain times. So instead of giving a knee-jerk response, and slashing price tags, Hyundai slashed risks instead, and put its workers to promoting a no-strings-attached refund if shoppers lost their job in next 12 months. As a result, the company's sales doubled in January 2009, while the industry's plummeted 37 percent, the biggest drop in 50 years.

CULTIVATE EMPATHY AND EFFECTIVE LISTENING ABILITIES

The best way to create positive change, and promote teamwork and innovation, is to think *FASTER*, and stay keenly attuned to your environment and respond to changes within it more rapidly and productively. But without possessing empathy, it's hard to relate to the needs of your customers and coworkers; hear their voices; engage these individuals; or move them to take positive action. And without cultivating effective listening skills, it's hard to stay attuned to shifts in the market, cultural trends, and competitive landscapes. Similarly, without applying emotional intelligence, it's hard to lead people; change direction; or respond quickly and effectively to emerging trends as they develop. Worth keeping in mind: According to The World Economic Forum, 90% of top performers boast better abilities here than peers, and studies show that without them, it's difficult to become a successful leader. In effect, the better a listener and more empathic an individual or organization you are, the likelier you'll be to adapt and succeed in record time going forward.

TURN FLEXIBILITY INTO FUTURE-PROOFING

Look closely, and you'll notice that corporate giant MasterCard no longer calls itself a "financial services" business. Instead, it refers to itself as a "technology and innovation company" – one that's dedicated to relentlessly engineering and reengineering solutions designed to meet shoppers' fast-changing needs. Likewise, other multibillion-dollar organizations like Allstate Insurance now live by core values that include consistently leveraging customer insights, data, and technology to create disruptive innovation; executing well-considered decisions with precision and speed; and focusing relentlessly on those few business activities that provide the greatest impact as well. As Allstate notes, it's important to "be a learning organization that leverages successes, learns from failures, and continuously improves." The more you adopt similar outlooks in your own business, the simpler you'll find it to stay relevant, and in tune with even fast-changing times and trends.

FOCUS ON BUILDING RELATIONSHIPS AND DELIVERING TOP-NOTCH CUSTOMER SERVICE

Word of mouth is today's most powerful form of advertising, existing customers are easier to sell to than new ones, and creating meaningful, long-term relationships is the secret to standing out and finding lasting success in business. (Case in point: Bain & Company found that raising customer retention rates by just 5% can help you increase your profits from anywhere from 25%-95% - a massive windfall.) In fact, building long-term relationships can also be key to survival. Back in 1994, popular software creator Stardock was a small, independent studio making products for IBM's short-lived OS/2 operating system. Treating buyers like trusted friends, if product release dates slipped though, they'd actually send shoppers free copies of other products as a surprise way of saying "thank you" for their patience. Building that goodwill was a smart move: By 1997, the OS/2 market had collapsed, as did company revenues. Quickly switching gears to the Windows market, the business needed to raise funds fast: So it pre-sold its new product (*Object Desktop for Windows*) as a $50 one-year subscription. But for the first year, *Object Desktop* was little more than a concept sketch. However, customers – who'd migrated from OS/2 to Windows by the thousands – remembered how Stardock had treated them and purchased it by the thousands. As a result of this groundswell of support, the company not only quickly turned the ship around – it went on to create many other hit products.

The bottom line: Unless you've got a crystal ball that works, it's hard to predict the future with 100% accuracy as a modern executive. But when you apply the skills and strategies above, you'll always discover more effective ways to keep up with competitors and keep in tune with even the most disruptive and unpredictable business markets.

X. HOW TO FUTURE-PROOF YOUR BUSINESS

Contrary to popular belief, future proofing your business doesn't have to be difficult, time-consuming, or expensive. Nor is coming up with future proof ideas as hard as it sounds when you make a point of regularly planning ahead in business. As briefly touched on earlier, and the *FASTER* operating model reminds us, discovering how to stay relevant is largely a process of consistently making simple, evolutionary changes versus chasing revolutionary leaps forward in business. Following, you'll find seven simple strategies that can help you fast-track growth and innovation, and give your organization all the capabilities it needs to stay ahead of the curve.

1. Listen to Your Customers – As discussed previously, customers are the most reliable source where organizations looking to future-proof themselves can routinely turn to discover winning new ideas. Ironically though, less than a third of businesses today have formal solutions in place for actively tracking the feedback that shoppers are sending, let alone translating it into actionable strategy. Tools such as polls, surveys, questionnaires, market research, and social media monitoring software (for tracking popular topics and conversational trends) can all help you surface invaluable insights here. But if you truly want to successfully mine today's most consistent source of winning business ideas for great concepts, including clever and cost-effective ways to stay relevant? It also pays to embrace the concept of "open innovation," or regularly putting out calls for help to partners, suppliers, and even the general public. In effect, the more you invite input from outside sources of every kind, the more you can radically multiply the amount of insights and resources available to you – and the speed at which you can solve any challenge.

2. Encourage Employees to Speak Up – As those closest to customers on a running basis, external-facing workers of every kind (e.g. sales reps, customer service specialists, community managers, field service technicians, etc.) are often an organization's most well-informed audience. Therefore, if you want to future-proof your business, it's also vital to find ways to tap into their insights at every turn. Noting this, it's no surprise that today's most successful businesses don't just make a point to put platforms and programs in place that facilitate teamwork and collaboration, and give workers a greater voice in making decisions, across the board. They also actively work to promote cultures of trust and respect in which everyone is encouraged to speak up and share their input, and reward contributors for bringing both potential opportunities and challenges to the organization's attention. Likewise, to build and maintain competitive advantage, these firms consistently provide their people with the systems and support that they need to quickly translate ideas into action – and make leadership a concept that scales at every level.

3. Freely Collaborate with Peers. Want to move faster? Make a point to flatten lines of communication in your enterprise, and allow information, insights and support to flow freely throughout your organization. The more readily you can align tools, talent and resources toward achieving common goals, the more readily you can foster innovation. Case in point: Germany's Association for Chemistry and Economics (VCW) has over 30,000 members spread across hundreds of industries. Knowing that teamwork would be crucial to successfully managing change, and accelerating the speed at which it could adapt, VCW wanted to create a solution that would allow these members to more easily connect and collaborate to help drive ongoing innovation on a huge scale. So the organization coined the concept of "Social Chemistry" and built a website that allowed members to crowdsource ideas, team up with talent from outside the field, and pool resources across public and private organizations. Within just 5 weeks, the VCW had produced hundreds of ideas, sparked dozens of new initiatives for the industry, and helped identify several trends which weren't even on the association's radar. Ask yourself: What's stopping you from doing similar?

4. Spread Your Risk – Leading organizations don't try to be risk-free, but rather risk-averse, and actively pursue a more calculated range of business bets. As with financial portfolios, these enterprises constantly manage and adjust a portfolio of strategic ventures. Not all wagers will pan out. But all are designed to collectively help the organization grow its capabilities, spread risk, and learn through real-time monitoring and course correction. For example: Market leaders like Sony and Microsoft specifically commit teams to pushing the boundaries of technology in new directions, knowing that these new developments may be put to a variety of useful business purposes — not all of them commercial. Similarly, in good times, your organization can also plan for bad times by routinely rolling out new ventures and solutions that offer the potential for evolution, growth, and expansion as well. Market leaders are constantly using innovation laboratories and incubators to play a portfolio of investments and wagers. You can do the same.

5. Iterate, Don't Reinvent – Innovation isn't always about coming up with game-changing concepts. In fact, simple shifts in communications or operations strategy can be every bit as successful at helping you create huge windfalls for your business. Ask yourself: How could you reuse existing resources, capabilities, or solutions in new and exciting ways – or repackage them to appeal to new audiences? What could your organization do in a single step that's currently taking it several steps to perform – or where could technology help you automate or skip these steps entirely? In essence, innovation (like future-proofing) is largely a matter of perspective, and process of constant reimagining and reinvention. The more frequently you make a point to challenge yourself and your people to think differently, the more innovative (and, ultimately, future proof) you'll be.

6. See Tomorrow Today – If you want to stay competitive, and learn to move *FASTER*, don't just focus on competing with rivals' present-day offerings. Also regularly consider where the future is heading, the way in which end-users' needs are constantly changing, and how you can put solutions in place today that tomorrow's customers will demand. Rather than simply keep pace with rivals, top innovators always consider where the future is heading and strive to put the solutions tomorrow's audiences will demand in place today. For instance: Google, HP and 3M are famous for encouraging employees to invest large portions of paid time exploring fresh ideas and experimenting with new innovations. As opposed to standard maintenance and upkeep tasks — i.e. research, marketing, member services, etc. — how much of your organization and its staff's time are you investing in long-term growth activities designed to expand its reach and capabilities? To help bridge the gap from here to there strategically, provide workers with the freedom to take lots of small, cost-productive risks that have the potential to pay off for the business from a long-term perspective, learning as they go. Similarly, on an organizational level, make it a priority to play a portfolio of new strategic ventures at all times, optimizing and course-correcting as you gather and learn from market feedback along the way. Remember, not every new venture will pan out. But just by pursuing this process of constant evolution, you'll help actively grow your business' capabilities and insights, and improve its ability to shift with changing markets over time.

7. Challenge Every Assumption – Ironically, if you're still doing things the way they've "always been done" on the job, it pays to remind yourself: As fast as today's business world changes and evolves, odds are that they are no longer the best way to still be doing them. Keeping in mind that competitors are always looking for ways to do things better, faster, and cheaper, it's crucial to routinely challenge your people to look for ways to proactively disrupt yourself before you get disrupted by other parties. That's why it's important to always be experimenting with new innovations and solutions, as above, especially while things are going well, and you can most afford to take risks. The more you make a point to actively push yourself to try new approaches or strategies, and challenge longstanding assumptions, the more future-proof your business (and its ideas) will ultimately be.

Ultimately, building a future-proof business, and determining how to stay relevant, isn't about having all the answers up-front. Rather, it's about being more open-minded and resilient, and taking a *FASTER-*thinking approach to your operating strategy – as well as remaining self-aware enough to know when to rip up and/or rewrite the plan as you go.

XI. SUCCESSION PLANNING:
HOW TO GUARD AGAINST UNCERTAINTY

Learning to expect the unexpected is a time-honored rite of passage for every business leader. But according to surveys by RocketLawyer, 72% of executives currently have no succession plan in place defining how to handle leadership transitions if they should find themselves unable or unwilling to continue managing their enterprise. As a result, if you want to keep steadily and speedily pushing forward as an organization, in addition to getting in the practice of anticipating uncertainty, it's even more important to make a regular habit of thinking ahead at every turn, and having a well-defined backup plan ready in case unforeseen disaster strikes.

Just ask New-Jersey-based BioAegis Therapeutics, whose co-founder and chief scientific officer Thomas Stossel (brother of famed TV personality John) suddenly and unexpectedly passed away at age 78 on September 29th. Not only did the 10-person firm suffer a major personal and professional setback in the loss of the former Harvard Medical School professor, whose pioneering research was responsible for the discovery of plasma gelsolin. (A naturally-occurring anti-inflammatory protein that helps regulate the body's immune system to better fight off disease, and whose unique properties the company has based its treatments upon). It was also forced to contend with these unforeseen developments at the most inopportune time, with fundraising efforts for the firm's Phase IIb clinical trials – spearheaded by Stossel – scheduled to begin just days later.

"Everything came out of left field," confesses chief operating officer Valerie Ceva. "Tom was a healthy guy in great physical shape who didn't have an ounce of extra fat on him... we were just in shock." Luckily, she explains, the company was prepared to weather the storm, having specifically been structured in such a way as to continuously capture and share internal learning; maintain strategic flexibility; and leverage the talents of employees whose knowledge, skill sets, and experience overlapped. It was these foresights, mapped out and planned for since day one, says Ceva, which allowed the firm to remain resilient despite adversity, and keep moving ahead, even in the face of potentially show-stopping setbacks.

"We found out about Tom's passing late on Sunday night," she says. "By 8A Monday morning, the management team was on the phone and revising its strategic and communications plans. An hour later, employees knew what was happening, and we started reaching out to our our support network of advisers and experts. Within a week, numerous individuals had stepped up to help take on Tom's different responsibilities and fill in any strategic gaps. Shortly thereafter, we were back to going full steam ahead."

However, as executives remain keenly aware, BioAegis' successful perseverance in the face of unexpected hardship is more uncommon than not. All-too-often, as noted in our bestselling book *Make Change Work for You*, business owners or operators are too focused on dealing with the here and now to plan for tomorrow today. Likewise, prioritizing thinking up smart ways to successfully hand off leadership duties to others isn't necessarily second-nature for those who've helped build an organization from the ground up.

Whatever the reason – whether too hands-on, too short-term-oriented, or too reluctant to give up control of their enterprise – executive leaders are often too absorbed with other priorities to give long-term planning proper attention in their business. According to surveys by Wilmington Trust, nearly eight in ten blame being too preoccupied with managing their firms' day to day operations for this oversight. Likewise, four in ten say that they're too busy to get around to the task, or that potential business hand-offs sit too far ahead in the future to justify the time and resources they'd spending mapping them out in the present. But whatever your reasons may be for failing to formally map out a succession plan, delaying the process is a big mistake that can cripple your enterprise's chances of future-proofing itself, suggest market leaders like PNC Financial Services. Rather, the firm notes that it's imperative for business leaders to always have a Plan B ready in case of illness, disability or death, and an exit strategy in place if they're planning to retire.

"You can't predict or plan for every eventuality," seconds Chris Zimmerman, management consultant with FutureProof Strategies. "But you can certainly prepare yourself and your team in advance to greet many common challenges that businesses face, and exert greater influence over those outcomes that are within your power to control. Making a point to actively think ahead and plan around uncertainty is becoming an increasingly important principle for any business owner to embrace in today's growingly unpredictable business world."

Happily though, given how increasingly volatile the market is becoming, more and more business owners and operators are currently making a point to adopt this philosophy, and build succession planning into the fundamental DNA of their workplace. For example, custom software maker Menlo Innovations, who applies the *FASTER* model to solving the challenge by pairing two employees together at every PC in its office – and switching these partners weekly. It's a system that founder Richard Sheridan says is designed to help rapidly facilitate knowledge transfer amongst employees, expose team members to new business approaches and angles, and break down the walls which often isolate potential collaborators. Moreover, the methodology allows employees who possess unique insights – and often become so busy that it's hard to share their vision, field every request, or take time off – to avoid becoming bottlenecks to productivity, and enjoy better work-life balance. But perhaps more importantly, by ensuring information disseminates amongst coworkers, it also serves as a ready failsafe in case that employee elects to retire, or move on to another firm.

"In today's working world, where businesses and careers are more fluid than ever, nothing should ever be considered permanent," suggests Zimmerman. "Having a succession plan in place can help you protect your business from whatever unforeseen twists, turns, and happenings that the future may bring."

Bearing this in mind, experts recommend taking a more forward-thinking approach to business strategy if you want to lay the groundwork for your firm's continued success, and creating a winning succession plan, including:

  • Cross-training employees in similar skills, and ensuring that information is freely shared throughout your enterprise, so that no operating process or professional relationship is dependent on the efforts and insights of one single person. For example: All scientists at BioAegis are capable of standing in for one another when performing experiments, and Stossel himself made a point of collaborating with myriad clinical partners to ensure that others were well-versed in his signature techniques. Using a similar system, you can build in layers of redundancy that can help safeguard your organization in the event of an unforeseen loss or departure.

• Encouraging workers to communicate often and freely with others in your enterprise. This includes both holding weekly meetings to ensure colleagues are kept up to date on various initiatives' progress; briefing peers on current tasks and workloads; and using online storage tools to document and share all work performed and business insights gained from its performance. That way, if you need to hand projects off to others, they'll be able to quickly pick up where you previously left off.

• Creating a broad organizational support system and actively working to partner with external parties or organizations to multiply the number of resources and insights you can draw upon. Case in point: Over the years, BioAegis' built a network of expert advisers and supporting cohorts at leading academic institutions and government agencies worldwide. Because of this advance planning, the company was able to quickly staff back up when it needed to find someone to fill an outstanding role or tackle an unassigned task on-demand, e.g. those Stossel had previously fielded.

• Promoting a culture of support, teamwork, and encouragement, and actively espousing the values of collaboration to your workforce, so as to help keep information from being siloed off inside the enterprise, and more rapidly train all of its available resources on solving problems. That way, not only do employees become more actively vested in the company's success, but also willing to consider other perspectives, and capable of working more effectively together to respond to challenges more creatively.

• Engaging in routine strategic planning exercises, and challenging yourself and your staff to come up with answers to multiple what if? questions. In addition to making sure you've covered competitive bases like how to respond if certain market events or actions by rivals come to pass, also be sure to account for prospective legal and financial considerations. Increasing regulation, governance, and oversight may all impact your industry in coming years: Having a plan in place that allows you to effectively respond in turn could be crucial to adapting.

"Make a point to block out time in your schedule to start thinking about tomorrow now," advises Susan Levinson, CEO of BioAegis. "No matter [what size] your business is, you always need to be planning for the future. Thus with [any given] loss, a team can readily shift focus from addressing concerns about how to fill gaps to fielding questions about how to best honor a given individual or organization's legacy."

.

>*BEING UPWARDLY MOBILE:*

PUTTING YOUR CAREER ON THE FAST-TRACK

I. THE NEW MODEL FOR CAREER SUCCESS

Constant change is the new status quo and uncertainty the only certain in business. This radical instability fundamentally undermines the foundation of traditional career advancement models, grounded in stable organizations, working environments, and job hierarchies to ascend. To ensure ongoing career growth and progression going forward, tomorrow's leaders won't just need to be more skilled and capable. They'll also need to move *FASTER* – and be more forward-thinking, resilient, and able to improvise as well.

As interviews with scores of leading business researchers, academics, and senior leaders at leading startups and global innovators such as Cisco, Merck and Dell reveal though, this concept is seldom instinctive. Rather, it requires working professionals to anticipate continuous career disruption, and take calculated steps to acquire elastic skills – widely-applicable talents which can easily be remolded to fit any industry, organization, or job role. Capable of serving as springboards to future opportunities, these elastic skills can allow workers to become more flexible, agile, and adaptable regardless of circumstance, even as knowledge and experience steadily compound. They can also help executives rebound more effectively from unexpected setbacks. But perhaps most strikingly, the process of gaining these skills, and the invaluable insights, contacts, and experiences that often accompany them, frequently requires one to execute a series of seemingly counterintuitive career moves – often at the expense of immediate opportunities for advancement or financial gain.

To understand the new model for career success, I interviewed more than 125 serial and self-made successes, including a mix of intrapreneurs, entrepreneurs, and leadership training professionals, to see how they both fueled ongoing success in their career and prepared future leaders to greet tomorrow's challenges. As I explain in bestselling book *Make Change Work for You: 10 Ways to Future-Proof Yourself, Fearlessly Innovate, and Succeed Despite Uncertainty*, feedback indicates that the new formula for career success is simple:

- Stay ahead of shifts in your industry by constantly broadening your experience and perspective.

- Cultivate flexibility and resilience in your career.

- Be a generalist, and learn as much as you can. Learn how to learn.

- Assume that disruptions will occur, and prepare for them in advance.

- Equip yourself with the skills and resources you need to improvise.

- Be purposeful and forward-thinking about the choices you make.
- Use feedback gained from the results of your efforts to keep making more informed choices going forward.

As a simple example, one successful marketing executive we polled guards against career upheaval by taking smart risks. To accelerate growth, and become more adaptable, he routinely reviews his professional strengths and weaknesses then takes on a progression of carefully-chosen job roles that address any shortcomings, and provide compounding education and experience that serve as launchpads to future opportunities. He specifically seeks out job positions that require him to exercise new professional skills, and present him with more challenging roles and responsibilities, which allow him to grow in ability, gain new talents, and demonstrate competence in unfamiliar areas over time. This makes him more flexible and attractive to future employers, and capable of self-sustaining should he ever need to operate independently. To circumvent the onset of potential career disruptions, he routinely disrupts himself, gaining the knowledge, training and elastic skills needed to successfully adapt long before the future arrives.

Assessing survey participants' success strategies, it quickly becomes apparent that three new career moves that are equally elastic as the skills they can convey – the *sidestep*, *backstep*, and all-important *slingshot* – can further help executives sustain upward momentum, even in uncertain times. If you find your career plateauing, you can move sideways, a.k.a. sidestep, into a position of equal rank and pay (into an organization that offers more opportunities for advancement or career growth) or take a *backstep* by moving down the ladder and accepting a less-prestigious title or less pay (say, leaving a Fortune 500 business to work for a start-up for the chance to gain new skills and hands-on experience, or work in emerging markets). Alternately, you can take a slingshot by making both a sidestep and a backstep while staying focused on your ultimate career target: When you apply the knowledge, experience and skills gained through these moves, you'll leap far ahead.

Case in point: The executive I interviewed recently left Google to join a small, unproven start-up offering him more challenging opportunities in a more demanding role and business environment. Just over a year later, he returned to Google, vaulting himself several rungs up the ladder in terms of rank and pay via this process.

But equally important to contemporary career success as becoming more resilient is cultivating the ability to sustainably improvise. Sheryl

Sandberg, author of popular book *Lean In*, suggests that the pathway to career success is a jungle gym you must traverse erratically, rather than an upward ladder to climb. However, this theory is incorrect, as it presupposes that rungs (stable, predefined opportunities, e. g. available job positions) exist to climb upon and that others have placed them there for you to utilize. Feedback from the executives I polled indicates that the process of scaling current career heights is, in fact, more like free climbing up a sheer cliff face. To ascend it, you'll constantly have to carve out your own handholds (i.e. create your own hands-on learning or job opportunities) and cling to convenient outcrops for leverage as you climb (make the most of whatever limited resources are available to drive forward momentum). Likewise, you must continually assess the odds of success for each prospective career move along the way and make the strategic choices that convey the most long-term, sustainable benefits (e.g. skills or insights you can use for a lifetime).

When career hazards bar forward progress, you cannot simply expect to find a rung conveniently placed nearby, nor is it always advisable to grab the closest one at-hand. Instead, sometimes you must circle around or even double back on your chosen route to reach your ultimate career objective. As *sidesteps*, *backsteps*, and *slingshot* maneuvers reveal, sometimes, this means having to assume a less-advanced job title in a different department (or even take a pay cut) to learn new skills or switch roles or organizations to boost opportunities for advancement. To maneuver around unexpected stumbling blocks or dead-ends, all you can do is keep weighing the odds, considering potential payoffs, and picking the most promising new trail to follow. What's more, the only safety harness available is one that must be self-created. But if you look to the future, plan ahead, and consistently make intelligent bets that help you acquire the elastic skills, connections and resources that pave pathways to further opportunity, you can create the professional equivalent of a Bungee cord that can save you if you ever slip, and—as you begin to bounce back—also help vault you to unexpected heights.

Here's a simple illustration. One young technology executive we interviewed graduated during the Great Recession with minimal business experience and qualifications. Skeptical of a graduate degree and low-paying, dead-end jobs' ultimate value, she used the *FASTER* model to create her own shortcut to career success by turning her life into a self-guided MBA program. Committing five years to tackling a semester-like timeline of self-imposed challenges, including launching new conferences and entrepreneurial ventures, she purposefully declined full-time employment to pursue self-directed goals that filled in gaps in her experience and skill set. Effectively, this young professional bet that the experience, skills and professional contacts she'd gain by undertaking these exercises would outweigh a measly, entry-level paycheck.

***

>> >> *EXERCISING RESILIENCE AND IMPROVISATION CAN HELP SUSTAIN CAREER GROWTH, EVEN IN THE FACE OF CONTINUED SETBACKS* >> >>

***

Taking a *FASTER* approach to career advancement, not only did she complete all her goals far ahead of schedule, and gain talents and knowledge far beyond those possessed by most peers. She proceeded to found a successful online start-up, become a noted industry thought leader, and serve as the youngest-ever member of her college's board of trustees. She says she made far safer bets than peers who passively fell back on traditional career advancement systems. Win or lose, she knew she'd increase her confidence, capabilities, and value to prospective future employers with each successive attempt.

Wherever you sit on the career spectrum, exercising resilience and improvisation – and adopting a *FASTER* mindset – can not only accelerate career growth, but help sustain it, even in the face of continued setbacks. Consider the following examples, which demonstrate the power of elastic skills and career models at work.

Three albums and a thousand shows into a thriving music career, the drummer for the gold-selling band Gravity Kills should've been living the high-life. Instead, his band was owed thousands in unpaid sales, and he was living on his wife's $24,000-a-year day job. When his publisher went bankrupt, he leveraged his love for music, ear for acoustics, and an architecture degree he had into a burgeoning career building high-end performance spaces for clients like Washington University, the St. Louis Art Museum and CBS Radio.

A successful biologist realized that he loved the social aspects of the discipline more than its scientific aspects, so he put himself through law school, only to realize six years later that it wasn't a good career fit. Carrying over elastic skills he'd acquired throughout these career shifts (including a flair for strategic planning, research, and corporate communications) into new disciplines, he now uses them to serve clients in myriad fields as the head of a thriving association management business.

Two basic principles – being proactive, purposeful, and persistent with regard to one's objectives, but highly flexible with strategic approaches – are central to modern career advancement. As researchers Siobhan O'Mahony and Beth Bechky explain through the concept of *stretchwork*, winners don't simply seek out jobs that pay the bills. Rather, they select specific occupational roles that can help them parlay competency in existing disciplines into new areas, and expand their toolbox of professional talents and capabilities, becoming more adaptable and resilient as they go over time.

Finding career success isn't about instant gratification. It's about constantly building bridges to future opportunities. As the heads of FedEx and Shell's most innovative leadership training programs suggest, the following principles can also help you sustain positive growth, even in the most highly-disruptive business environments:

• Become essential by seeking out capabilities, insights, and training that are inherently rare and difficult to come by. The more uniquely value-adding you are, the more difficult you become to replace. As a simple illustration, you might become your company's go-to expert on resolving complex regulatory issues or IT security challenges.

• Anticipate change and change with it by consistently striving to gain on-the-job knowledge and skills that will be in-demand tomorrow today. Know where you wish to be in your career. Then consistently push yourself to learn, grow, and expand your abilities and comfort zone by pursuing opportunities that can help you get the elastic skills that can help you chart a course to this destination, however roundabout its path may be.

• Create your own luck by taking steps to put yourself in fortune's sights more frequently. Instead of exercising tired job skills time and again, look for ways to pick up new skills, or put those you already possess to new and novel purposes. Actively experiment with new business solutions, push the boundaries of your problem-solving abilities, and partner with others to spark innovation. The more you exercise your creativity, the more creative you'll be.

• Don't clock out when the workday ends. Put off-hours when others shut down to work towards your advantage by pursuing side-projects or interests that can help build experience, education, or helpful business skills.

• Differentiate by making your work portfolio your resume. That way, the next time an HR rep asks for your qualifications, instead of handing them a piece of paper that describes your experience, you can have something tangible you can point to and say "I did that."

In the same way that organizations must perpetually change and innovate to keep pace with changing circumstances and markets, so too must working professionals. To deal with impending career changes—expected or otherwise—it's essential to improvise, and think *FASTER*. You can better equip yourself to do so by seeking out the tools, training, and expertise you need to succeed long before you need them, and consistently applying these solutions to positive effect. If you're adequately prepared to greet impending changes, the rest is all about being ready, willing and able to change as situations dictate.

II. HOW TO ADVANCE WITHOUT BECOMING A MANAGER

So you've paid the cost, but don't want to be the boss? Fair enough: If you'd like to advance more rapidly in your career, you can choose to manage projects or become a subject matter expert instead.
To take the former path, attach yourself to high-impact and/or high-profile new ventures that are priorities for the organization, and push your skill set, comfort zone, and capabilities in new directions. For example: You might help your law or accounting firm launch its debut blog and editorial strategy; software company roll out its first-ever hardware device; or marketing firm transition to campaigns powered by analytics, not gut instinct.

If you can prove to your employer that you take to tasks readily and excel at (a) discipline (b) multitasking (c) time management and (d) problem-solving skills – and can be resourceful with limited resources – good things will happen. For instance, you'll:

• Carve out a level of respect and autonomy in your role

• Become a go-to resource for your employer

• Cultivate talents you can add to your professional toolkit

• Enjoy greater recognition from clients and colleagues

• Better position yourself to springboard to new opportunities when they inevitably arise

Such a career track isn't always straightforward, and you can't predict with certainty when a new opening or role may require the services of a promising recruit such as you. But using the *FASTER* model, and applying a number of career-enhancing accelerants, you can absolutely put yourself in opportunity's path more frequently. The best way to climb the corporate ladder is to stop waiting for others to promote you and promote yourself. Sometimes, you've got to sacrifice seniority, job titles, or temporary pay boosts – i.e. by making a lateral move into a more cutting-edge role with better growth opportunities in your organization – to get ahead in the long run. But thinking ahead has its own rewards. You can get ahead without having to lead people by routinely seeking out upwardly-mobile projects that grow your skills, boost your visibility, and provide more chances to show senior leaders you've got what it takes to excel.

Alternately, the second path to the penthouse suite is to make yourself indispensable to the enterprise, and so damn good that (a) others can't help but notice you and (b) you can't be replaced. Want to be your organization's resident expert on coding artificially intelligent tools, building blockchain solutions, or solving complex global logistical challenges? This is the job path for you. Because rest assured – if someone else can easily perform a task, deliver similar work product, and doesn't mind managing people as much, your days are already numbered.

Luckily, this latter route to the top (while admittedly more challenging, since it requires embracing hard tasks that others shy away from) can also help you take your stock up a notch and create more job security. In effect, if you're the salesperson that clients adore; the engineer with the specialized know-how to work with advanced technologies; or the only one who's learned to speak Mandarin fluently at the office? Your services will be in demand – and you can often charge a premium for them.

>> >> THERE ARE MANY WAYS TO REACH THE TOP, INCLUDING SEVERAL YOU CAN USE TO ACCELERATE CAREER SUCCESS BY TAKING A MORE SELF-DIRECTED STRATEGY >> >>

In essence, the more that you provide services and solutions that are difficult and expensive to replicate and serve as a crucial link in the value chain for your enterprise, the more chances to advance (and appreciation) that you'll enjoy.

Of course, becoming your firm's go-to cybersecurity pro or expert on complex regulatory concerns isn't simple. Getting ahead doesn't just mean investing in gaining additional skills, learning, and experience today. It also requires you to proactively seek out the talents and training today that will be in demand tomorrow. But the more you speak up, volunteer, and seize opportunities to expand your horizons – especially during off-hours when others are clocking out to go skiing in Vail or play on their Xbox One – the more competitive advantage you'll build, and faster you'll obtain it.

In the end, being assigned to manage increasingly large groups of people and tasks remains the most common way to advance in today's job market. But these days, there are many ways to reach the top, several of which can involve taking the road less traveled. Consider it a welcome development for those who'd prefer not having to wonder if John's going to call in sick the day before deliverables are due, or Jane's forgotten to fax those darned TPS reports again.

III. HOW TO GET COLLEAGUES TO LEARN & GROW

Consider yourself flattered if colleagues consider you a go-to guy/gal at your organization, and a go-to resource anytime they're in need of help completing a task. But as you've likely also discovered by now if so, excelling on the job can be both a blessing and a curse (not to mention exhausting), unless you learn to set some helpful boundaries up-front.

Mind you, doing so doesn't always come naturally to those of us whom aim to please and be liked. And certainly, we all want to help our colleagues out. (Who couldn't use a little extra good karma, and you know what they say about paying it forward...) However, it's important to remember that as working professionals, we are all operating with limited time and resources these days. Actively encouraging peers to be more proactive is a must in the modern working world if you want to move *FASTER*, especially if you're playing with a tight schedule.

To start with, remember that "No" is not a dirty word, and you don't have to feel bad about saying it – even more so if you can say it in such a way that peers can empathize with, and that actively helps speed others along in their quest.

For example, we all know what it's like to be under the gun. A simple "Apologies, I'd love to help, but I'm heads-down on a number of time-sensitive projects at the moment" or "OMG, that sounds like a great project... unfortunately I just don't have the bandwidth to take it on right now" can help set relatable expectations with others that you're unavailable to assist. But any time that you say no, you should also say yes to helping others find ways to help themselves by also offering a helpful suggestion, tidbit of advice, or piece of insight that can ultimately help them move further down the path towards accomplishing their chosen task.

For instance, you might couch subtle hints on how to solve a challenge in the form of leading questions. (Ex: "But have you tried reaching out to Jim? This is right in his wheelhouse;" "Did you check our new plug-and-play accounting tools yet though? They're great for this type of task;" or "You might want to pinging the digital marketing team, however – I know they're working on something similar.") Clever suggestions can help you politely help them arrive at helpful conclusions faster or steer them in more productive directions.

Alternately, you might also suggest making an introduction or two ("Do you know Jane Welles? She's been doing research into similar subjects") or looking at a useful resource. ("I don't know the answer off-hand, but our customer service recently team put together a FAQ that answers many frequently asked questions along these lines, which might come in super handy...")

On the flip side, in the case that someone comes to you for help, but seems stumped, you might ask some guiding questions.

- Have you tried X/Y/Z, by chance? (Googling it, checking this market research report, checking in with the IT, team, etc.)
- What do you think the best solution is? (Offering additional prompts as needed, i.e. "Is this something HR might be able to help out with, or you might find answers to on our online employee learning portal?")
- Did you try running it by [insert individual, department, or team name here] yet – they may have some helpful suggestions?
- What is the client/team suggesting? ("A few ways you might try weighing and reviewing options might include 1/2/3, etc.")

Of course, entire books have been written on taking control of your time and signaling to others that you won't always be available for them to fall back on. Some common suggestions include:

- Setting specific office hours when you're available and closing your door and turning off your phone's ringer when not.
- Putting away or out of office messages on your email and only responding to correspondence at predetermined times each day (e.g. 2-4PM, when you've gotten most of your tasks for the workday done already).
- Turning off instant messengers and chat programs when you need to stay focused and uninterrupted on work.

Ultimately, success here comes from (a) not being readily on-call anytime (b) teaching colleagues to be more thoughtful (c) taking command of your own schedule and (d) encouraging more proactivity on peers' part. Of course, helplessness and indecision are often symptoms of insecurity. The more you let your associates know that their work is trusted, give colleagues the authority and room to make decisions, and reinforce smart decision-making with praise and recognition, the more you'll help create and reinforce a workplace culture of self-sufficiency.

After all, while we all take pride in a job well done, there are only so many you can functions that you can perform yourself (and directions that you can be pulled in) in any given day. And the more opportunities that you give colleagues the room to learn, grow, and boost their experience and skill sets? The *FASTER* your enterprise will be able to consistently move – and better off your team, organization, and blood pressure will be.

IV. WHY YOU SHOULD PRIORITIZE SUCCESSION PLANNING & KNOWLEDGE TRANSFER

What's the best way to help your organization prepare for a valuable employee's retirement (and keep moving forward), especially if they're reluctant to pass along the knowledge they've gained over the course of their career? Someday soon, robotics and artificial intelligence solutions (so lifelike now that organizations are replicating entire individuals' knowledge bases and personalities with computers) may very well make this question obsolete. But until the machines take over – yes, we saw *Terminator* too... yikes! – a distinctly more empathetic and human approach is often called for.

***

>> >> *TO ACCELERATE GROWTH AND PROFESSIONAL DEVELOPMENT, CREATE REGULAR OPPORTUNITIES FOR COLLEAGUES TO SHARE THEIR EXPERTISE*>> >>

***

If you're getting pushback here, perhaps the answers lie not within a change of strategy, but rather one of presentation and pitch. For example, rather than simply asking an employee to document and record their learning and insights for business purposes outright, create opportunities and excuses for them to share their expertise instead. Some ways you might go about gently approaching the topic include:

• Arranging for the senior employee to serve as a mentor for up-and-coming leaders, or new interns and hires, on a consistent and running basis. (Hint: It couldn't hurt for the organization to spring for free lunch or breakfast when these get-togethers occur.)

• Incorporating the potential retiree into cross-functional committees, task forces, or project groups charged with affecting positive change, innovation, and finding ways to streamline, optimize, or improve workplace operations. Older and wiser, it's often nice to let them know you respect their opinion – and that you're providing opportunities for their voice to be heard.

• Offering new hires or junior employees the opportunity to "shadow" and learn from the more experienced worker by keeping pace with them as they go about performing the day-to-day duties of their job role.

• Making your longstanding hire a subject matter expert or thought leader of note, and asking them to help multiple videos, articles, whitepapers, blogs, etc. – each of which could later be used as training courses or guides.

• Assigning your experienced worker to projects and programs that require joint efforts between groups of people from different backgrounds and experience levels. The more time that all individuals get to spend with each other, the more all will learn from one another, more new perspectives they'll see – and the more new ways and approaches of tackling tasks that all will discover.

• Inviting the soon-to-be-retiring worker to participate in on-the-job events such as executive retreats, planning sessions, hackathons, etc. where they have a chance to speak up and share their feedback and insights.

• Pairing the individual with organizational education and development teams working on engaging learning tools such as video courses; interactive programs; 3D simulations; etc. as a trusted advisor and consultant to help incorporate their insights into and shape featured content.

• Encouraging young workers to conduct "informational interviews" you're your potential retiree about what the senior worker's role, responsibilities, and workload entail, and ask lots of smart questions – including about their best hints, tips, and advice.

• Asking your longstanding employee to be a guest speaker, panelist, or workshop presenter at internal or external events – especially those that encourage them to lead and guide others through instructional exercises or scenario-based challenges.

• Providing part-time or flexible work opportunities for the party considering retiring, which may help ensure that their learning and insights are available for the organization to draw on and learn from for longer than you expect.

It's no secret that people are a business's greatest asset – and that the most experienced people are often the most valuable sources of insight within the enterprise. If you want to encourage them to pass on their learning and wisdom, then it pays to remind them of just how important that their expertise truly is to your organization – and create myriad opportunities to spotlight and underscore it for the benefit of everyone involved.

V. HOW TO RECRUIT & RETAIN TOP TALENT

Contrary to popular belief, the fastest way for your business to attract and retain top performers that can help you achieve your goals faster isn't to throw money at the problem. Not only are Millennials and Gen Zers more motivated by opportunities to learn, grow, and build lasting careers than a paycheck. They're also increasingly drawn to businesses who champion innovation and making an impact in the community, and consistently equip workers with the skills and insights needed to succeed in tomorrow's workplace.

Consider that an estimated shortage of 18 million high-skilled workers is expected globally within the next two years, and top performers will soon be as choosy as actual employers when it comes to hiring. Finding the right hires will soon be more important than ever too, noting that research indicates that high-performers are 400 percent more productive than their peers. Keeping these challenges in mind, when looking to attract and retain top talent going forward, don't just create favorable benefits packages for them. Also strive to create a welcoming and supportive environment that emphasizes personal growth and learning to attract tomorrow's top working professionals.

When hiring and interviewing job candidates, no matter the role, make a point to highlight where opportunities to grow and advance exist with the organization. A few desirable skills you can both look for when recruiting to help you identify top performers, and that you can help tomorrow's leaders gain and exercise over time include:

Interpersonal Communications – The ability to effectively write, speak, and listen is an essential talent to possess when it comes to leading, interpreting, and giving direction. Likewise, a sense of emotional intelligence is also vital: Employees need to be able to understand where others are coming from so that they can better empathize and act on this information, especially if you're looking to put them in management positions.

Multi-Tasking – Today's working pro is often involved in multiple projects, tasks or initiatives – the ability to adroitly juggle all will be increasingly essential to possess going forward. Tomorrow's workers must be well-equipped to manage multiple tasks, and complete work efficiently, correctly, and with a minimum of stress, despite being pulled in many directions.

Dynamic Decision-Making – Effective problem solving requires the use of both creativity and logic. Workers with solid problem-solving skills won't just be strategic thinkers that are capable of objectively interpreting information. They'll also be capable of keeping a cool head under duress and acting thoughtfully when a solution is needed.

Organization – Possessing the self-disciple to effectively gather data, conduct research, and keep tasks both well-managed and on-schedule will be important traits for any leader going forward. Gaining them can help job candidates be better managers and contributors, and more efficient and productive in their roles.

Pro tip: Once you've identified prospective hires, to create more compelling job offers, it often helps to analyze your ideal hire's needs and customize benefits to each candidate. Likewise when working with the best of the best, it's also important to remember that top performers may come and go – part of the normal employment cycle when working with such in-demand hires. After all, these leaders are often eager to take on new challenges and roles and acquire skills in new areas and industries. If a top performer desires to part ways with your business, by all means, make an offer to retain them – but also don't be afraid to let them go if need be. These same workers may very well return to your company at a later date, wiser, more experienced, and armed with greater insights that can help you succeed.

Essentially, finding more ways to work *with* peak performers – not just have them work for you – is the secret to attracting and retaining top talent. The more you can create win-win opportunities for everyone, the happier and more successful both you and they will be.

VI. WHEN YOU SHOULD TALK ABOUT SALARY DURING HIRING

Money is often an awkward topic of conversation for many professionals hoping to climb their way up the career ladder – let alone do so with a quickness. Even more so while you're busy trying to make a positive impression with and catch the interest of a prospective employer. Luckily, following a few simple guidelines can help you make the numbers add up without coming across like you're all about the bottom line.

For starters, early in the interview process, the focus should be on building awareness and relationships, and convincing employers that you're the right man/woman for the job. While courting them, keep the focus on making a good impression, and helping others get to know what makes you a compelling and unique job candidate. If you shift the focus of conversation to finances and away from your key selling points and the fundamental value that you can bring to an organization before others have bought into the concept of you coming on board? You run the risk of spooking prospective employers, who may feel that the cart is being put before the horse, or pricing yourself out of an opportunity before you've had a chance to make a compelling case for yourself. It's wiser to wait to broach the subject of money once you've had a chance to set yourself apart from other job seekers, line up some allies and advocates, and given future colleagues a chance to know you better.

***

>> >> SET YOURSELF APART FROM COMPETITORS FIRST: MONEY SHOULD BE CONSIDERED AS A SECONDARY TOPIC OF CONVERSATION>> >>

***

Once you've had a minimum of a couple interviews, and received signs that a company is interested (hint: inquiries re: references, start dates, future interviews with specific higher-ups, etc. often prove helpful indicators), you can begin to broach the subject of money. However, it should be considered as a secondary topic of conversation. More important during this phase of the hiring process is to first convince potential employers that you're excited about the role and opportunity, and motivated by other factors than cold, hard cash. Now is a good time to talk about the responsibilities that might come with the position, types of projects you'd be contributing to, opportunities for growth inside the organization, etc. Having established your genuine interest in the role and firm, you can then afterwards transition into discussions about salary.

A helpful way to broach the subject is to ask several questions about the position you've applied for, its responsibilities, whom you'd be working with, and other related topics, making compensation just one of many subjects of discussion on the list. Alternately, you can wait until employers take the lead here and bring up the matter for conversation. Do be prepared prior to all interviews and have a preferred salary range in mind (online searches, compensation reports, surveys, and discussions with peers can all help in your research) in case the topic is raised, however. Likewise, be prepared to negotiate: It's important to both do your homework, so you know the facts up-front, don't price yourself too low or out of an opportunity, and demonstrate a willingness to be flexible. And be prepared to stick to your guns. Knowing what you're worth; being able to talk specifics in terms of your strengths, skills, and experience; and having facts at-hand that definitively demonstrate the benefits that you can bring to the table can help you command greater value.

Again, the sequence here for fast-tracking success is simple:

• Create a positive impression, and help others come to understand what makes you the right fit for the role.

• Demonstrate your passion for the position, and why you'll be a great addition to both the team and organization that's hiring.

• Let money be a topic that naturally flows from other sources of discussion, and don't rush to fast-track it to the top of the list.

• Research and equip yourself with the insights you need to negotiate from an informed position, and make a point to highlight specific examples of the value you can bring when it's time to discuss salary.

• Leave yourself room to negotiate, and remember: From better benefits to more flexible work hours and greater learning opportunities, there are many ways to structure a package that works for you, even if you're offered a lower starting salary.

• Before you pull the trigger and accept a job offer, make sure to get anything you've negotiated in writing.

Granted, money isn't everything in business. But by applying a little more strategy to the job application and hiring process, you can help the question of dollars make more sense for all parties involved.

VII. WHEN YOU SHOULD TALK TO YOUR BOSS ABOUT A JOB OFFER

Whether you love your job or wish it would go the way of the fax machine and Palm Pilots, keep in mind, the circumstances surrounding job offers from other companies are often open to interpretation (hint: your boss will always wonder who initiated the exchange) and once you let the genie out of the bottle, you can't put it back.

It's typically unwise to share your news with superiors unless you have a signed offer in hand and plan on pursuing it, in which case they deserve at least two weeks' notice. As for your colleagues, a similar heads-up is advised—once you've spoken with your manager first. With colleagues, though, you needn't be as specific with details on the new position. In any event, should you receive an offer you plan to decline, you're best served staying silent and keeping the information on the down-low. A good question to ask yourself if you're considering revealing that you've received overtures from another firm before sharing this information with others at your workplace is as follows: What message might it send that I'm even bringing up the topic?

In theory, loyal and satisfied employees aren't the sort to typically point to an interest in entertaining outside proposals. Likewise, even passing comments to this effect may impact team morale, productivity, and peers. Colleagues may disappointed, taken aback, or even jealous, while superiors may question your commitment to your role and where your loyalties lie, or be concerned about the signals that it sends to your coworkers.

Even if you plan to decline the offer, letting colleagues know you have an offer out there before you've accepted it may, at best, be considered in poor taste. At worst, it can come across as bragging, or a calculated attempt to negotiate more favorable terms from your employer. No matter the actual circumstances surrounding your receipt of the offer, be advised: Bringing up the topic will inadvertently cause others to consider the concept of your departure (realistic or otherwise), and this may lead them to be more skeptical and less open and/or trusting. However, if you've received an alternate job offer, and would prefer to use it as a means to negotiate with your employer rather than leave your current position, you might bring up the subject for discussion privately with your superior. Be aware, though: Doing so may very well strain relations with your boss and you may risk offending your employer. Going in, it may provide some comfort to know that many companies have downsized and are in lean mode already, meaning that if you're still on the books, you're considered an important contributor. However, you have to be careful not to overplay your hand here either. Competing offers can suddenly be withdrawn, and if you operate in industries where competition is high (media, public relations, advertising, etc.) and many job candidates are available, you may have less leverage than you'd like.

If you choose to go this route, the key is to do extensive research upfront. Before you ask your employer to counter a competing offer, take time to consider precisely what it is you're looking to gain (more money, additional responsibilities, reassignment to other teams/ projects, etc.) in your negotiations. Likewise, it's important to be flexible. Going in, have a few points that won't trouble you much to concede on, but will make your employer feel as if they've gained some ground by obtaining these concessions.

***

>>>>LEAD WITH POSITIVITY AND KEEP DISCUSSIONS STRICTLY TO FACTS, NOT EMOTIONS>>>>

***

When approaching the topic with your employer, lead with positivity, and keep discussions strictly to facts, not emotions. Explain what you love about your current company and role, how you'd like to progress within them, and where you feel room for constructive change exists. Be prepared that conversations may not go as planned though, and that you may need to part ways with your present employer, in which case it's best to do so on amicable terms. After all, it's not uncommon for working professionals to leave a company to gain new insights and experience, only to return to their former employer in a new role at a later time.

If you do need to give an employer notice, try to end things on as high of a note as possible. When communicating, stay positive about your company, colleagues, and time with the organization, and don't make negative or critical comments about them. Being respectful and helping with the transition—e.g. by offering to bring others up to speed on accounts or train new hires—can help promote goodwill.
And remember, you're not obligated to share extensive details on your

new job (just that you've found another position), and shouldn't put contact information for it in your outgoing email signature. Rather, use that space to let folks know whom to contact in your place at your former employer, and use personal contact information if they'd like to follow up on non-work-related matters instead.

VIII. HOW TO APOLOGIZE WHEN YOU SCREW UP AT WORK

Alright, so you screwed up and missed a deadline, blew a presentation, or otherwise dropped the ball at work. It happens to us all, but if you take accountability and learn from the mistake, it doesn't have to be the end of the world, or derail your path towards career advancement. Granted, apologies can be difficult. But when presented sincerely and in well thought-out fashion? You may be surprised at how quickly you can transforming a negative experience into a teachable moment that builds teamwork and trust amongst all parties involved.

First, a few ground rules to note:

- Apologizing is not a sign of weakness on the job.

- Taking responsibility can be a way to demonstrate strength – and that you're aware of an error, are taking steps to fix it, and remain both capable and in control of any situation.

- Over-apologizing for minor hiccups (i.e. showing up two minutes late for a meeting, or forgetting to drop your coffee mug in the dishwasher) is unnecessary when a simple "I'm sorry" will suffice.

- You'll want to avoid making frequent, extraneous apologies to avoid the appearance of being insecure.

That said, some common scenarios in which apologies are warranted include:

- Neglecting to perform an assigned task.

- Failing to provide insights, feedback, or deliverables by assigned deadlines.

- Delivering work product that is not up to specifications and standards.

- Snapping at or otherwise speaking out of turn to a coworker.

- Undertaking actions that inconvenience employers or potential employers, e.g. if you accidentally sleep through an interview or flub a new business pitch.

- Providing incorrect or insufficient information to colleagues or clients.

• Inadequately preparing for workplace scenarios and situations.

Each apology you make will be unique, and must take into account both the context of the error and perspectives of all parties involved in the gaffe. However, saying "I'm sorry" on the job doesn't have to be as difficult as it seems if you acknowledge your mistakes and exercise a little more thoughtfulness in terms of next steps. A few simple rules you can follow for making each expression of remorsefulness count:

• **Take time to stop and think** – If it's a large error you've made, or important transgression, give yourself and others time to calm down, process the situation, and consider an appropriate response.

• **Don't let issues fester** – Apologize as soon as possible (preferably immediately following the hiccup if it's a minor transgression) so as not to give others time to jump to conclusions or misread your intent.

• **Accept responsibility for your mistakes** – Restate the issue, claim ownership of the mishap, and make it clear that you understand what went wrong, so as not to give the impression of insincerity.

• **Validate others' feelings** – You may disagree with these opinions, but it's important to respect their positions, which will promote understanding and empathy while minimizing conflict.

• **Don't make excuses** – Avoid using words like "but," "however," or "if" – take blame, acknowledge the shortcoming you've engaged in, and explain why you agree that it was wrong.

• **State how you'll fix the problem** – Make it clear why the concern won't arise again, and the specific steps you're taking to correct it, whether this means checking in with supervisors more frequently or seeking regular feedback from peers. Then follow through promptly on these action steps.

• **Be considerate when making contact** – Big and/or sensitive mistakes should be discussed and dealt with face-to-face; lesser offenses might be handled via a hybrid method, including an emailed apology note with an offer to meet and discuss issues in-person if they'd like to chat further. A sample email template that can help is as follows:

Hi Jamie,

Hope you're doing well. I just wanted to take a minute and apologize for forwarding the most recent draft of our research to the client before you'd weighed in. I thought I was being proactive, but I realize that I should have checked with you first. I apologize sincerely, and I've instituted an online approvals and review process with our communications and IR teams so that it won't happen again. Is there anything else I can do to help get things back on track? I'd be happy to discuss at your convenience.

Sincerely,
William

Ultimately, the best way to handle a mistake is to promptly and positively address it, learn from the scenario, and move on. Apologizing can be an uncomfortable process, but the more you lean into it, the easier it becomes.

IX. HOW TO CORRECT YOUR BOSS APPROPRIATELY

They say the customer is always right. But your boss? Not so much. However, calling out a supervisor when they've misspoken or got facts wrong can be a touchy subject.

The last thing you want to do is embarrass them, or come off as either being insubordinate or a know-it-all, which means the best approach for addressing a manager's mistake is to take a light touch. Seven simple rules can help you do so if your boss isn't big on feedback:

1. Do Your Research – Double-check your facts (noting that managers often have more up-to-date or comprehensive information at their disposal) to make sure that an error has actually been made before speaking up.

2. Pick Your Battles – Consider whether or not the correction is worth potentially crossing swords over. Ask yourself: Will it make your boss look foolish or out of touch? Will it prove costly to a client or the company? If it's a minor gaffe – e.g. a small detail they've misquoted – perhaps it's best to let it slide, or "coincidentally" pass a research report or infographic your manager's way via email that "may be of potential interest."

3. Consider Your Motive – Are you rocking the boat just to be a contrarian, or nitpicky? Will bringing this matter to your supervisor's attention really create positive change for your colleagues, clients, and the organization, or is it a superfluous gesture just to "set the facts straight?" If there's not a compelling reason to challenge your manager, don't.

4. Time Your Comments Smartly – Picking the right time to discuss matters with your boss is vital, especially if you require their full attention and anticipate having a difficult conversation. Avoid approaching superiors out of the blue, while they're busy or preoccupied with other matters, or in the middle of group gatherings to maximize the chances of them having a better reaction to receipt of this information. Of course, if a time-sensitive and critical problem stands to emerge as a result of their actions, it also pays to be proactive. Urgent requests to connect can be made, e.g. via a quick face-to-face ("Hi Don, would it be possible to get together today at 5PM – I've got a time-sensitive matter to discuss?") – but don't ambush them around the office coffee pot.

5. Speak Privately – Do not confront your boss in public in front of coworkers and clients, or in a public place where there's the potential to be overheard, so as not to embarrass them. Instead, schedule time for a private chat and have a safe forum ready (i.e. a nearby closed-door meeting room) in which to hold the discussion.

6. Make Helpful Suggestions – Never tell bosses they've "made a mistake" or are "wrong" and don't make demands or attempt to give instructions. Instead, couch comments politely as helpful ideas, insights, and problem-solving suggestions that guide them to arrive at similar conclusions, and suggest like-minded ways for addressing areas of concern. Rather than simply point out mistakes, offer clever ideas for implementing corrections – your goal should be to spark constructive dialogue around any topic.

7. Practice the Art of Acceptance – Bosses won't always agree with you, and you won't always be able to change their mind. And if they decide it's time to move on, and end discussion surrounding the topic, or stay the course the way they'd way already defined? It's time to gracefully accept their decision and move on. (If someone's safety or wellbeing is genuinely at stake, however, it may be time to take up the discussion with someone else; hopefully your human resources department has guidelines or procedures for reporting and resolving these kinds of concerns.)

Whatever the outcome of these discussions, if concerns are major, you may wish to document and make note of the fact that you've raised red flags in case of future issues. But bosses are human too: When politely approached with insights that they may have made a mistake, and given a graceful opportunity to correct it, they often will – and be grateful for your feedback and support throughout the process.

X. HOW TO BREAK BAD NEWS AT WORK

Like the erstwhile philosophers The Rolling Stones are fond of reminding us, you can't always get what you want. That's especially true at work, and goes double for employees sitting far down the executive totem pole. Decisions made at the top are often the final word on a subject, and may not be the word the rest of the organization wanted to hear.

Have to spread the word about an impending layoff, drop the ball about a reduction in benefits, or sell the idea of a merger or corporate reorganization? Got to break the news that long-awaited promotion won't be forthcoming, or that there's going to be a drop in billable hours? These types of operating changes are often among the hardest to explain, and the hardest to empathize with as a middle manager. And though the decisions may be what's best for the organization, they might very well be among the least popular decisions with employees. So how do you deliver news to colleagues when it's not the news they were hoping for, or news you're keen on delivering? The answer is threefold: Be short, be straightforward, and be empathetic. While never easy to get the message out, you'll find that being honest and respectful with coworkers is the best policy.

Here are a few simple guidelines you can follow to help achieve better results for all parties involved:

Be Prepared – Sit down with your own supervisors prior to connecting with your subordinates. Go over the questions your team is likely to have about the information, and the meaningful and substantive responses you can give. Have any important documentation—fact sheets, charts, etc.—ready to go in advance of discussions with colleagues receiving bad news; and ensure the materials are designed to clearly and simply present information in an understandable manner.

>> >> *BEING HONEST AND RESPECTFUL WITH COWORKERS IS THE BEST POLICY* >> >>

Be prepared to take time to walk through all the changes with your team. Determine when and where to best break the news, and the context in which you can do it most humanely. A casual coffee with team members away from the office, for example, might feel more appropriate than a series of one-on-ones at your desk. And practice breaking the bad news (hint: a video camera can help with the critique) before delivering it, as body language and non-verbal cues can influence others' reactions. It pays to be calm, confident, and factual, while also empathetic—no one wants to come off like a robot here.

Uphold Your Bosses' Decisions – It's important to maintain your composure when conveying others' wishes. Do not contradict organizational choices that you disagree with, and maintain respect for those who have made the decisions. Let colleagues know how much care and consideration went into these choices, and that decision-makers considered other options extensively before concluding what they felt was best for the enterprise.

If workers are aware you don't concur with these choices, be upfront about it. You can always say it wasn't the choice that you might have made, but that it's what leadership has decided is best for the organization, and that you'll work with colleagues to do your best to implement these updates. And make certain your direct reports know that the door remains open for you and your team to offer suggestions and insights to the leadership team as you go about the process.

Don't Skimp on Details – The vaguer you are with your team, the more disconcerting things will be for them. As best you can, provide hard facts that help explain the rationale behind any given decision and its coming impact. If details haven't been discussed or provided to you by upper management, or you're not at liberty to share insights at this time, it's ok to say so—and point out that you'll continue to seek answers as situations evolve.

Likewise, it's important to let colleagues know that you remain at their disposal to help with any additional questions that they may have. Be sure to offer reassurance wherever possible as well: It's natural for human beings to assume the worst, especially in the absence of other insights. Any helpful perspective and positive feedback you can offer will be of assistance, provided the insights are grounded in hard fact. If things aren't certain at the moment, offer whatever information you do have, and details on when more information might be available.

Set Expectations – Be clear about the fact that a decision has been made, and make it apparent that you won't allow others to waffle when it comes to implementing these choices. Be direct and upfront about what you will and won't expect employees to do once you've put the word out. (For example, you might expect that they *will* reach out with further questions and keep forging ahead, while expecting they *won't* fire up the rumor mill or start worrying when there's no impending need to.)

Provide clear parameters about how and when it's ok to vent, noting that workers will undoubtedly want to blow off steam on the heels of unpopular decisions. And don't allow yourself to be boxed into answering questions or offering assurances that you don't have the facts or the authority to support. It's better to let others know when you don't have an answer, and that you'll be back in touch once you've had a chance to do more research and follow up.

Face it: No one wants to be the bearer of bad news, especially when it's a decision they disagree with. But sometimes the best way to handle things when they don't go your way, and you don't have the power to amend them, is to simply go with the flow. With any luck, you'll eventually get the opportunity to present new facts and feedback that offer a more ready chance to change the situation.

->LEVELING UP:

MAKING TECHNOLOGY WORK FOR YOU

I. HOW TO STAY COMPETITIVE IN A CONNECTED BUSINESS WORLD

Goodbye, Internet of Things, hello, Internet of Everything. With over 7 billion devices now connected and communicating online, according to IoT Analytics, and 2.5 quintillion bytes of data generated every single day, the shape of today's marketplace is being transformed before our very eyes. How can your organization adapt to these changes, and stay competitive in a world where customers are constantly providing feedback and markets evolving in real-time? Simple – by adopting a *FASTER* mindset and making data-driven design and flexible IT infrastructures the cornerstone of your business strategy.

With the growing advent of 5G, automation, robotics, and other emerging technologies, learning to more effectively capture, analyze, and capitalize on data in real-time will be increasingly vital to success going forward. For business leaders, it's not just about finding ways to get better at collecting information – it's also about learning how to become more adept at using this information to quickly make smarter decisions. To thrive in coming years, modern executives should start by considering the following insights with regard to data – the basic building block upon which successful business strategies will be built. As a rule, if you want to plan for growth, it needs to be: (1) Accessible on-demand (2) Freely and securely exchangeable between solutions and (3) Able to infinitely scale. For senior executives, this means having to both build flexible IT infrastructures capable of supporting these goals, and big-picture operating strategies that allow you to function more adroitly on multiple levels.

Following, you'll find a number of hints, tips, and strategies that can help you innovate, lead digital transformation, and fast-track your way to unprecedented growth using data-driven strategies:

1. Take a Long-Term View – Start by thinking about data and all the ways in which it can be leveraged to support your organization: Could another division, department, or business venture benefit from the information you're capturing? Likewise, when crafting an IT infrastructure and data management strategy, consider the many ways in which this data can be applied to achieve a variety of larger goals – not just the immediate objectives at-hand. To maximize data's impact, don't just design IT support systems with the capability to constantly capture insights and info and apply information gained from past exchanges to present user interactions either. Also build them with the capability to tap into external sources of information (e.g. third-party plug-ins or information feeds) as well. A cornerstone of innovation, it's imperative to craft data management solutions that enable you to successfully capture and leverage information in myriad ways, and across a wide spectrum of activities, to fuel rapid and ongoing growth.

2. Get Your Whole Team Onboard – From a leadership and management perspective, numerous individuals from numerous areas of an enterprise with differing perspectives and priorities are often involved in making IT decisions. To reconcile these disparities without compromising your ability to maneuver – e.g. promoting agility and innovation without sacrificing cost-efficiency or risk management – get stakeholders from all areas involved in the process, and promote open communication and teamwork among them. Creating cross-functional teams can help you facilitate collaboration, and design data and IT solutions so as to better support a broader range of individuals and activities. By sharing information and insights, you can gain deeper insights into your organization's current and future needs, and more effectively train resources towards common goals in order to fast-track completing them.

3. Start with the Finish in Mind – Businesses often build new high-tech solutions first, then try to figure out what IT and data management needs are required to support these ventures afterward. Instead, take the opposite approach and determine what resources you'll need to support these ventures, and how to best structure your data management and IT architecture, before crafting new apps, products, or services. Ask yourself before designing any new solution: Have I considered its characteristics and functions, and crafted a data and IT infrastructure that properly aligns with the needs of the effort I'm trying to promote? In addition, when designing high-tech offerings, remember that any solution that you create will generate data; benefit from ingesting additional insights from other sources of information (requiring you to build with widespread compatibility in mind); and need to scale as time passes.

4. Iterate, Don't Reinvent – Many industry leaders often start digital transformation or innovation efforts with an established base of data management and IT tools in place already. Rather than throw these preexisting systems out, and start from scratch, to move FASTER, look for ways to steadily iterate and build upon them, slowly rolling out new business functionalities a little at a time. For example: You might start by adding an online storefront to your website before implementing a complete end-to-end inventory management and returns system. Similarly, you might provide targeted promotional offers to specific groups of customers before launching marketing tools that track individuals' purchasing habits and personalize unique offers to them. Remember: Changes to your IT operations don't have to be big or expensive. Begin by determining which simple tweaks could make the biggest impact on your business, then take an incremental and layered approach to implementing new solutions to improve the odds of successful roll-outs.

5. Expect to Grow and Expand – Today, IT infrastructures that offer endless uptime; flexible design blueprints (e.g. those that support hybrid/multi-cloud and on-demand operating environments); and unlimited business growth are the gold standard. Noting this, any high-tech tool or framework you implement in support of modern business operations should adhere to specific guidelines. For one, all should be contextual – able to use data insights and historical reference points to provide personalized interactions to every user – and capable of functioning without hiccups. (Zero downtime is the gold standard, with organizations now thinking more in terms of disaster avoidance as opposed to disaster recovery.) Similarly, any apps and platforms you implement should be based upon distributed operating architectures so as to ensure always-on, high-speed performance, ensuring that interactions happen quickly and in real-time. Likewise, all solutions should be designed so that they're easy to update, expand upon, and have no limits on their ability to grow with your business.

As you can see, organizations operating in every field face significantly growing data management and IT challenges going forward. But finding ways to get ahead in tomorrow's more challenging business environment doesn't have to be time-consuming or difficult when you apply a few simple shifts in thinking and perspective. Some helpful questions you can ask yourself as you go about crafting your organization's IT backbone that can help you move *FASTER* in coming months: Have I chosen a high-tech architecture that allows me to quickly shift strategies, and add features and functionalities as needed? Is it compatible with a wide variety of high-tech tools and systems? Are apps and platforms I've built able to easy interface with other solutions? The more you consider similar concepts, and plan around them, the better-positioned your business will be to stay competitive in the years to come.

II. 5 WAYS TECHNOLOGY CAN HELP YOUR BUSINESS STRATEGY

From cutting-edge online payment solutions to smartphones as powerful as PCs and cloud-based work productivity tools that let your desktop travel wherever you go, technology now makes it possible to do business anytime, anywhere. Likewise, with businesses of every size set to spend more on digital transformation than ever before, it's clear that more and more organizations are also turning to these high-tech tools as a way to future-proof their enterprise. Happily for modern executives wondering exactly how technology will change the shape business in the future, it's not hard to get a sense of where the virtual world is headed, and how you can tap into it to stay ahead of the curve. Here, we take a closer look at five major shifts in business that technology is set to usher in within the coming years, and how these sea changes can help you future-proof your organization, as well as take its productivity and performance to the next level.

AI, Analytics, and Predictive Insights – So much for operating in silos. With billions of devices now connected and talking to one another, according to World Economic Forum, there are now 40 times as many bytes of data in existence online as there are stars in the sky. Likewise, research firm IDC suggests that over 463 exabytes of data will be generated daily worldwide by the year 2025 (the equivalent of hundreds of millions of DVDs). That's a massive amount of work productivity tools and information that business leaders can tap into to find out details on customer preferences and purchasing habits and provide more targeted offers in turn. Likewise, it's an incredible volume of data that they can be scanning to better assess risks, determine where to place strategic bets, and leverage to create uniquely-customized products, services, and solutions that better speak to individuals or target audiences. Paired with cutting-edge analytics and artificial intelligence (AI) tools, not only can your business use these advances to quickly find a wealth of ways to better collect, manage, and leverage data that can help you make smarter decisions. You can also use these futuristic advancements to target ads and offers to viewers at the times they're most receptive to them, and even predict what tomorrow's shopper wants before they know themselves. Not only can technology now give you all the tools to translate every customer interaction (online or off) into crucial insights. It can also give you the visibility and input needed to rapidly translate these indicators into winning business strategies.

Virtualized and Mobile Workforce Management – With over 2.5 billion smartphones now in circulation worldwide, online shopping having overtaken retail spending, and 63% of companies now using remote workers, even as global competition continues to skyrocket, the writing is on the wall. Mobile, remote, and virtualized workplace and market environments are the future of business. Luckily for modern organizations, a huge range of high-tech work productivity tools and communications solutions offer simple, cost-effective ways to help you empower and field a virtual or remote workforce of any size. From videoconferencing solutions that can track your physical movements to apps for scanning and sharing documents and invoices, the best productivity tools for work will soon go far beyond cloud storage solutions, however. Just a few sample signs of how technology will change business in the future include artificially-intelligent drones that can be used to perform remote site inspections; interactive 3D training simulations that dozens of distantly-located colleagues can interact within in real-time; and robotic arms that surgeons can manipulate from miles away. Similarly, stores that let you pay for goods just by picking up an item and fleets of driverless transport trucks also hint at the many ways technology can help you transform business operations going forward. In short, high-tech solutions provide all the tools you and your teams need to connect, communicate, and do business 24/7/365 in tomorrow's world – and compete on a global scale.

Online Payments, Digital Transactions, and Automatic Billing – These days, it's all but given you'll be working with a growing array of partners, customers, and vendors all around the world. That means having to process transactions virtually anytime, anywhere, and in a growing range of currencies, with digital payments skyrocketing in popularity, and set to top $168.65 billion in transactions by 2026. Luckily, a variety of online payment processing solutions and automatic billing options can help you improve relationships with those you work with, and streamline operations across the board. Similarly, with credit card use at an all-time high, and high-tech advancements in finance growing, you can only expect to see these payment solutions becoming smarter. In coming years, they'll be able to enable wireless payments, process peer-to-peer transfers and transactions (so you can split bills with friends), and function as all-purpose digital wallets – modes of functionality your business would do well to plan for. Likewise, for those organizations hoping to future-proof themselves, it's worth noting that many firms are also now using high-tech payment solutions to save billions on fraud. For example, today's artificially-intelligent voice-monitoring tools can now be used to analyze shoppers' speech and mannerisms and verify their identity when they call customer support lines for help. Some are even smart enough to identify imposters and immediately report them to authorities, helping provide significant savings and avoid lost work productivity.

**

>>>>HIGH-TECH SOLUTIONS GIVE YOU THE ABILITY TO LET WORKERS GO HANDS ON WITH NEW TOOLS, STRATEGIES, SCENARIOS, AND SOLUTIONS TO SEE HOW THEY WORK, AND HOW THE RESULTS OF THEIR ACTIONS AND DECISIONS PLAY OUT IN REAL TIME>>>>

**

VR and AR Training and Education – With 74 million people and counting, Millennials (born 1981-1995) have now surpassed Baby Boomers as the single largest generation in the workforce, and Generation Z (which follows) is expected to surpass them in size soon after. However, both prefer interactive exercises, lifelike simulations, and hands-on training over traditional instructional courses and career development programs, and – like all of us today – they also now have an attention span shorter than that of a goldfish. Luckily, high-tech and highly-interactive work productivity tools such as virtual reality (VR), augmented reality (AR), and 360-degree video solutions provide more engaging ways to train tomorrow's leaders by example. These solutions give you the ability to let workers go hands-on with new tools, strategies, scenarios, and solutions to see how they work, and how the results of their actions and decisions play out in real time. Rather than describe scenarios in a hypothetical sense, such high-tech training options allow organizations to simulate environments and scenarios in realistic detail, and – depending how interactive they'd like to get – actually give applicants a chance to go hands-on and see how they fare in different contexts. It's the next leap forward in training from gamification: In essence, you can try on the shoes of virtually any career role and see how you fare, even in the most complex and demanding of tasks or environments – and it helps trainees boost learning and recall. Retailers are leveraging these tools to help customer service pros learn to deal with demanding situations, including irate shoppers and high-traffic sales days; educational institutes and healthcare companies are using it to train surgeons or medical students, offering them a working glimpse into the human anatomy; and hospitality, incentive, and destination marketing companies are using it to help workers take virtual tours of hotels, properties and other facilities.

Cyber Security and Analytics – Unsurprisingly in a world of online commerce, cybercrime is today's fastest-growing form of criminal activity. Set to cost organizations a whopping $5.2 trillion by 2023, virtually half of all businesses suffered a data breach just in the last year alone, making the need to future proof against online and high-tech threats an absolute necessity in today's digital world. Luckily, technology can help you guard against these growing threats (which include 480 new digital dangers released every minute), and not just in the form of free or paid virus-scanning tools. Rather, today's hottest new network-monitoring solutions are artificially intelligent, and can actually track every single user interaction and use these insights to create baseline models of how systems behave under normal conditions. Once these baselines have been set, they can then continually monitor your systems for any anomalies or suspicious behaviors – and shut these concerns down in seconds of detection. What's more, these high-tech tools also get smarter over time, and can even scan for and close system loopholes before they come under attack. Using these solutions, you can regularly scan all apps, systems, solutions, and devices connected to your network; conduct vulnerability testing; and instantly lock down compromised systems or accounts to quarantine the scale of any compromise. With the average cost of a data breach now hovering around $3.86 million (not counting damage to a business' brand or reputation), making a point to implement these measures will be critical to future-proofing any business going forward.

III. USING 5G TO TRANSFORM YOUR BUSINESS

Thanks to the rise of global high-speed wireless connectivity and supercharged mobile devices, market evolution now occurs at a pace that even high-tech pioneers could once scarcely have envisioned. But despite the multitude of disruptions – e.g. augmented reality, social commerce, the sharing economy, etc. – that technology has enabled in recent years, it bears noting. Such advancements are practically miniscule when compared to the sheer level of business innovation that 5G wireless networking technology promises to usher in.

Even more reliable than 4G LTE wireless networks, and up to 64X more responsive, this cutting-edge approach to data transmission (which leverages lightning-quick 1Gbps speeds to deliver near-instantaneous download times) won't just define the next decade. Rather, within just two years, 5G networking technology and the legion of always-on, artificially-intelligent apps it'll soon power will also prompt tomorrow's business leaders to fundamentally reimagine the very scale at which they function and operate.

In effect, not only will 5G networks enable fleets of mobile workers to seamlessly connect, manage multinational organizations, and disrupt entire industries from virtually anywhere they travel with a connected device. As the digital backbone behind tomorrow's most advanced high-tech infrastructures, they'll also power the next generation of smart cities, self-aware devices, and autonomous vehicles – just a few of many game-changing business applications.

Consider that according to Gartner, over 21 billion items will be connected to the Internet of Things by the end of 2020, with 5.5 million new ones going online each day. In addition, it's expected that nearly three-quarters of the workforce will be mobile (and nearly-three quarters of digital spending will originate from smartphones, tablets, and portable devices) within the next three years alone. As a result, leading consumer brands won't just potentially need to reconsider the very shape of products and services, as well as the high-tech backbones that they use to support day-to-day operations. They'll also have to redesign these solutions for speed and flexibility as much as cost-savings and performance, and consistently rethink how they leverage the tools that 5G technology provides (e.g. faster speeds, deeper data insights, and greater virtualization) to create more effective frameworks for powering tomorrow's most forward-thinking products and solutions.

"A driving force helping power crucial advancements from the Internet of Things to predictive analytics and machine learning on a massive scale, 5G is a true game changer," explains Jan Geldmacher, President, Sprint Business. "Not only does 5G technology create a wide variety of new opportunities for and open up new markets and business models to organizations of every size. It will also play a critical role in driving global innovation going forward."

Picture control rooms from which government leaders can direct citywide traffic flows, coordinate emergency relief efforts, and manage energy consumption across thousands of homes. Self-driving cars capable of scanning the terrain around themselves for miles, noting the position of every pedestrian, vehicle, and pitfall poised to cross their pathway. Factory floors manned by nimble robots that seamlessly work alongside humans, delivering unprecedented levels of precision and safety, even while sending productivity levels soaring. These are just a few of many potential applications for 5G networking technology that will transform tomorrow's business world – and help market leaders completely reimagine a dizzying array of industries from finance to manufacturing and transportation.

Whatever the field or potential application, implications are clear: Put simply, 5G networks promise to exponentially multiply the scope at which market leaders think and innovate.

"Using 5G technology, organizations can easily connect thousands of machines, data points, and sensors – and provide organizations with the tools and insights that they need to develop successful, forward-thinking global business strategies," says Geldmacher. "In just one simple example, look closely at what many market disruptors are doing with artificial intelligence and robotics, and you'll already see a number of revolutionary developments taking shape. These are the types of innovations that 5G encourages and enables."

Equally important, 5G technology's turbo-charged connectivity also blurs the lines between network, device, and software interactions so that organizations of every size can seamlessly hop between communications tools and commercial boundaries without pause. It also serves as an amplifier for smart computing and predictive analytics – allowing enterprises to more effectively process enormous amounts of information, anticipate market shifts, and juggle logistical challenges on a grander scale. And as more and more market leaders are growingly coming to realize, practical applications for the technology are seemingly endless.

Consider communications apps so advanced that they can answer customers' questions so quickly and accurately that clients with assume that they're interacting with live call service representatives. Alternately, imagine medical tools and equipment so precise and responsive that surgeons can operate in real-time on patients that are situated in hospitals thousands of miles away. These examples only scratch the surface of what's possible from a commercial perspective courtesy of this forward-thinking new technology.

"Going forward, just one of many things [companies like ours] aim to do with 5G technology is make it possible for robots and humans to work in hand," says Geldmacher. "We also want to empower artificial intelligence (AI) creations [computer programs capable of thinking like people] to contribute positively to society."

Equipped with 5G technology – which vastly reduces load times, and lets you download vast amounts of data in seconds – not only can top consumer technology brands now design and power thousands of connected devices. Leaders in myriad fields from finance to healthcare and retail can also piggyback on these innovations to create a new generation of more intelligent and responsive robots, apps, and electronics of every kind. Offering more widespread and reliable connectivity, advancements in 5G networking also make it possible for workers all over the world to more effectively collaborate together in order to build breakthrough ideas. Just a few high-tech revolutions you can expect in coming years will include a multitude of always-on, artificially-intelligent apps; hyper-intelligent robots and home solutions of every shape and size; and augmented and virtual reality tools that fundamentally change how we interact with our surroundings.

For instance, imagine self-aware cities whose artificially-intelligent minds can regulate traffic flows, coordinate emergency relief efforts, and manage energy consumption across millions of homes. Cutting-edge medical devices that can help doctors and nurses scan for the presence of injury or illness and successfully treat conditions in minutes. Factories staffed by robot helpers that can detect the presence of and seamlessly work alongside humans, sending productivity levels through the stratosphere. Or retail or restaurant settings in which all orders, deliveries, and customer service requests are processed by computer-controlled applications so real that you'd think you were interacting with another person.

***

>> >> *THE ARRIVAL OF 5G NETWORKS THREATENS TO EXPONENTIALLY MULTIPLY THE SCALE AT WHICH LEADERS WILL BE FORCED TO THINK AND INNOVATE*>> >>

***

Going forward, it's not implausible to imagine that both consumer technology leaders and 5G networking technologies will completely transform the shape of the business world. And, for that matter, that leading consumer brands may suddenly find their legacy and reach extended into other, more far-flung fields as they help leading players in a variety of commercial sectors reinvent a dizzying array of industries from manufacturing to finance and transportation. But more importantly, the dawn of the 5G age looks to usher in a time in which organizations will be given the chance to fundamentally reimagine the very scope at which they function and operate.

In effect, the arrival of 5G networks threatens to exponentially multiply the scale at which market leaders will be forced to think and innovate. These advancements won't just potentially enable brands (and the virtualized workforces which support them) to disrupt entire industries from virtually anywhere on the planet using a connected device. They'll also enable organizations to easily access thousands of connected sensors, devices, and data points – giving enterprises the tools and insights needed to pioneer groundbreaking solutions and strategies. Making it possible to seamlessly operate across far-flung locations and commercial boundaries, 5G technology essentially offers the possibility for brands to digest more data, predict market shifts, and tackle challenges on a far greater scale than they ever could at any point in history.

Computers that think like people and devices so intelligent that they can predict your every need are just the beginning, though. If 5G truly does deliver on its promise to offer a more agile and flexible platform for hardware and software development, it will provide a readymade springboard for innovation on a global scale. As a business leader, it's important to ask yourself: Are you ready for the coming market shifts 5G's arrival may usher in – and the many ways in which it can help you accelerate growth and innovation? If not, now's a good time to consider what disruptions the shift to a 5G world may bring, and how embracing it can help you both move FASTER, and stay ahead of the curve.

IV. HOW TO MANAGE CUSTOMER DATA MORE EFFECTIVELY

Operating and growing a successful business can be far easier than it sounds when you simply make a point to apply data-driven decision making more frequently. But with today's enterprise gathering more details and data from shoppers than ever before at every turn, finding ways to adroitly juggle a growing customer database – let alone translate its insights into *FASTER* and smarter business decisions – does take some advance planning and forethought. Luckily, a few simple shifts in thinking and strategy are all it takes for your business become more effective at customer database management, and more effectively handle the process of customer data analysis. Apply them to your IT and data management strategies going forward, and you can not only help your business get smarter faster, but also radically improve your ability to innovate and the speed at which you can make data-driven decisions.

1. Intelligently Filter – Talk about information overload: Over 2.5 quintillion bytes of data are now generated every day, with more than 90% of the world's online information having been generated in the last three years alone. Keeping this in mind, with websites, apps, and online solutions all now pushing more insights your way than ever before, it pays to be clearer up-front about which data points matter most to your business, and its data-driven decision making process. Noting that an average of 60-73% of all information in an organization goes unused for analytics purposes, it's important to focus on quality, not quantity here, and filter out less useful submissions. Start by determining which mission-critical variables – leads, sales conversion rates, purchase frequency, etc. – most readily map to improving bottom line results. Then implement customer database management systems and automated routines that allow you to quickly isolate and surface these details; track emerging trends; and quickly feed key insights to decision makers. As part of your auditing process, try to narrow things down to which 6-10 specific variables that, if improved, can make the largest positive impact on your business the soonest.

2. Collaboratively Scale – As the most fundamental building block of winning business strategies today, data can be applied in many ways to drive organizational growth and success going forward. Likewise, customer databases can multiply greatly in terms of usefulness when they're designed to be freely accessible to employees on demand, and to freely exchange information with other tools, apps, and solutions that you build. Keeping this in mind, when designing data management strategies, remember that customer information of use to one area or department of the business may also be of use to many other areas or departments as well. Likewise, colleagues of all sorts may be able to utilize these insights in a multitude of different ways. So to make smarter data-driven decisions here, it's vital to design a customer database management system that not only surfaces insights quickly, but is also designed to share best practices at an organizational level, and facilitate collaboration and teamwork at every turn. When plotting a shape for your IT infrastructure, think on a broad scale, and consider: Could others in the business benefit from having access to this information – and where else could customer insights be applied to achieve further objectives? In effect, your customer database should serve as a springboard to innovation. And the more you take a collaborative approach to customer database management and data analysis, and make a point to regularly share learnings throughout the organization, the more successful you'll be.

3. Stay Current – Incredibly, many executives estimate that nearly 30% of their customer data is inaccurate, with numerous business leaders suggesting that as much as half of this information may be erroneous. Bearing in mind how quickly customer details can become outdated, it's important to regularly update and refresh your database to stay current. To this extent, every 4-6 months, make a point to validate shopper details such as e-mail address, physical address, phone number, and other forms of contact information. Likewise, conduct a formal data audit to remove duplicate and non-working entries, and ensure consistency across all records. A number of intelligent and automated tools can help you scrub information, and keep customer details current. Similarly, your sales force should also make a point to sit down at review customer relationship management (CRM) tools and records at this point, making sure all notes and insights are up-to-date.

4. Centralize Systems – Not only is it crucial for a modern business to implement robust customer relationship management tools, especially if maintains a workforce of any significant size. It's also important to put unified and centralized systems in place that make it easy for workers across the organization (including representatives out in the field) to enjoy ready access to this intelligence on-demand anytime, anywhere. Being able to easily access these insights not only makes it much easier to do business on the go, and simpler to understand various customer segments and motivations. It also makes it easier to parse and understand any client's history at a glance, comprehend individual buyers' needs, and determine how to best tailor pitches or presentations so as to better connect. The more readily these insights and details can be called up on-command, and more rapidly you can surface key items of importance to prospective clients, the faster your teams can personalize and tailor recommendations and provide superior customer service.

5. Have a Governance Strategy in Place – In today's online and data-driven world, it's important to employ best practices in security measures to guard against data breaches and back up information on a real-time (or, at minimum, daily) basis. But in addition, maintaining proper customer database management today also involves having to put safeguards in place that can help you quickly defend against data compromise or corruption, and ensure high levels of network uptime. (With 99% or greater being the modern gold standard.) Similarly, to manage customer data more effectively, you'll also want to put formal operating policies in place that map out how data is to be gathered, stored, and archived, and how the process of disaster recovery will work in the event of a system failure or breach. Likewise, customers' data should be assigned a level of confidentiality, and access to this information limited to only individuals who need it to do their job at all times. Adopting a multi-factor authentication process (requiring multiple individuals to approve any change or update of note, whether to your business' methods of data collection or user access levels) can also help you better manage information and guard against compromise. With increasingly large volumes of sensitive data being shared online more frequently than ever, customer protection is also a vital topic to consider when thinking about how to effectively manage a customer database.

As you can see, data-driven decision making requires organizations to ingest, manage, and analyze more customer data today than at any previous point in history. But the process of effective customer database management, and customer data analysis, becomes much easier to handle when you design and structure your data management and IT governance processes to be just a little bit more resilient and robust.

V. PROTECTING YOUR BUSINESS FROM CYBER CRIME

As today's fastest-growing form of criminal activity, the numbers around cybercrime are staggering. Case in point: Over 480 new digital threats are released *every minute*, and nearly half of all organizations suffered data breaches or high-tech compromises in the last year alone. Incredibly, these virtual disruptions are expected to cost consumer technology market leaders over $5.2 trillion within the next two years – more than an entire world's worth of fires, floods, and other natural disasters combined. Worse, studies show it's not even criminals or hackers operating from outside your networks who pose the greatest danger to your operations. Rather, the biggest threat to your business today is expected to come from *trusted* sources: Internal employees, inside operators at business partners, or other users who already enjoy an approved presence on your systems and networks.

So how can business leaders hope to fight back, and respond to threats more rapidly, let alone in an age where the number of high-tech interactions, and amount of apps, transactions, and online exchanges that we're being asked to protect is skyrocketing daily? The answer lies in adopting a simple philosophy I call *Less Than Zero Trust* thinking – wherein it's assumed that not only is the first rule of cyber security to trust no one, but to not even trust yourself. Likewise, it also lies in adopting a range of both low- and high-tech security practices and measures designed to help your organization, as well as its people and partners, become familiar with exercising better security habits, and gain greater visibility into and control over network interactions. In effect, the more you ingrain a mindset of healthy paranoia in your staff, and the more you use advanced high-tech tools to defend your systems by constantly scanning for and predicting cyberattacks before they strike, the better at defending your organization from digital threats you'll be.

On the low-tech end, this means having to provide regular IT security training for every member of your staff, and grounding it in problem-solving exercises based on common real-world scenarios and newsworthy events. (Not to mention regularly refreshing this training every 3-6 months, and holding partners to the same standards.) It also means having to promote a culture of security in your business, in which users are skeptical of every request received – especially those that demand urgent attention, or warn of dire consequences – and take steps to verify these requests', and senders', validity through official channels. Likewise, greater security can be achieved here by tying multiple parties and layers of authentication to any financial transaction or user/system update of note. In effect, requiring two or more people to sign off on high-impact tasks allows you to minimize instances of human error, which is the single biggest threat to high-tech security today. After all, you can implement the best network security measures in the world, but all it often takes to circumvent them is just one phone call to con an innocent, unsuspecting employee into revealing compromising information that they shouldn't.

On the high-tech side, implementing a less than zero trust framework means regularly scanning all apps, systems, solutions, and devices connected to the network to ensure compliance with corporate policy. Likewise, it also means regularly subjecting all to vulnerability and penetration testing, and routinely reviewing user access privileges to ensure that people only have access to features and systems they actually need to do their jobs. (In case a breach occurs, in which it helps to lock down these accounts and limit exposure.) But these steps alone won't be enough to protect your business. You'll also want to make a point to invest in artificially-intelligent network cyber analytics tools, which use machine learning to scan networks, determine what passes for normal behavior or baseline activity, and report any anomalies. Using them, not only can you automatically get a level of real-time insight into what's happening on your system that's hard for users to hide from or disguise. You also gain the benefit of putting a self-improving security solution to work for you that can spot potential worries in a fraction of the time that IT pros can – and that can immediately act to quarantine or stamp out intrusions at their source when spotted.

Of course, keeping a modern business safe from network and data breaches isn't as simple as instituting training programs or installing even the most advanced software tools alone. Rather, it's a wholistic process that requires your organization to promote a culture of security and growth at every level, and engage in a variety of routine activities designed to help you stay one step ahead of the digital curve. More than anything else, education and proactivity are key to mounting a winning defense here, as is encouraging employees to step forward and speak up when they've spotted something suspicious, or fallen prey to a scam. The more you and your teammates actively work together to stay on top of cyber threats, and the tricks criminals use to deploy them, the better off you'll be. Likewise, the more you put technology to work on your side, the easier you'll be able to rest knowing that someone's looking over your virtual shoulder, and has your back, at every high-tech turn.

>>*UNLEASHING INNOVATION:*
STAYING AHEAD OF THE CURVE

I. WHY INNOVATION & REINVENTION ARE VITAL IN BUSINESS

Innovation in business is one of today's most widely-discussed topics. But while the term "innovation" is one of the most popular buzzwords working professionals hear today, it's also one of the most widely misunderstood. Many enterprises use it as a catch-all phrase to describe breakthrough advancements – e.g. cutting-edge new mobile and high-tech applications, products, and services. However, if you were to look in the dictionary, you may be surprised what you'd find. Innovation is simply defined as "the introduction of something new." By that same definition, it could simply be a new way to repackage or represent existing products or solutions, a new customer outreach strategy, or new approach to rebranding your organization.

Keep in mind that:

• Markets and competitive landscapes are constantly changing, as are audience expectations. Innovation helps organizations stay relevant, and stay competitive.

• Rivals are constantly rolling out and testing new solutions – and many can go from concept to execution in a month or less. Innovation helps us stay agile and forward-thinking, allowing us to constantly be experimenting with and updating business strategies to be more successful as we go.

• Modern market leaders don't just look to offer solutions that are competitive at present. They're also continually focused on delivering tomorrow's solutions today. Innovation provides a way to spot rising opportunities or challenges, stay better attuned to changes in the marketplace, and even predict the solutions that customers want before they know they need them.

But the best part for organizations hoping to be more innovative, and maintain a competitive edge, is that you don't have a tremendous amount of resources available or be a genius to get ahead in today's market anymore. As more and more business leaders are waking up and realizing, you just have to be a little bit more *resourceful* and *ingenious* instead. As noted, innovation in business merely refers to the introduction of something new. And while that something new could certainly take the shape of a game-changing new mobile/high-tech solution, it often pays to recall. Just as frequently it could take the shape of a new communications strategy, new pricing model, or even just a new way to reposition your business or brand to better speak to the needs of current or emerging audiences.

>> >> *TRADE SECRET: INNOVATION DOESN'T ALWAYS REQUIRE US TO REINVENT THE WHEEL* >> >>

***

In effect, simple tweaks in strategy and approach can often be every bit as powerful as revolutionary advancements in driving business growth and success. That's because, as countless scrappy young start-ups and forward-thinking companies in every field are proving, innovation doesn't always require us to reinvent the wheel – sometimes, it's enough just to give your proverbial tires a slight realignment. At heart, innovation is simply a process of constant learning and reinvention. And as research shows, the more willing you are to explore new opportunities and perspectives, and constantly be implementing and testing new solutions, learning as you go, the more successful your organization will often be.

For example, as a recent report by Aberdeen notes, it's not enough for enterprises just to offer dedicated mobile apps anymore. To be a market leader, you've also got to go one step further and offer end-users the kind of app that offers end-users a seamless, intuitive, and highly-customized experience – and that quickly and visibly saves them significant amounts of time, effort, or money. As Aberdeen's research suggests, top-performing organizations that prioritize these features and make a point to differentiate their solutions in such a way as to better help customers better meet their everyday needs are 10X more likely to satisfy users, and 4X more likely to see high mobile adoption rates. But adding this type of functionality to any of your solutions doesn't have to be a costly or time-consuming process. Just a few simple ways market leaders are finding to innovate and go beyond offering apps that provide baseline levels of functionality by using cost-affordable tools and technologies that are readily available right off-the-shelf, however, include:

> • Implementing voice-controlled assistants that learn users' habits to help save audiences time and trouble, and quickly route customers to subjects and services of interest.

• Providing highly-targeted and -customized offers, discounts, and specials to shoppers, including recommendations and suggestions that are trending amongst their friends and family members.

• Leveraging analytics tools and Internet of Things capabilities to monitor and even predict users' behavior, and serve up the features/products/solutions likeliest to resonate with them.

• Tapping into location-based services to share product info and let users comparison shop and find nearby retailers with goods in-stock right from their mobile device, or offer competitive offers right before they enter rivals' storefronts.

The good news for enterprises in every space is that an ever-growing array of solutions providers are offering a skyrocketing range of ready-to-go tools and technologies that you can quickly leverage or tap into, making innovation in business easier and more cost-effective than ever to achieve. Whether you're looking to implement platforms for driving innovation and facilitating collaboration across your enterprise, or more affordable and rapid ways to bring forward-thinking strategies and solutions to market, support systems are plentiful. The most successful innovation in business happens when enterprises and their workforces make a point to constantly reimagine and reinvent the benefits and value they provide. Happily, it's now simpler and more manageable to do so than ever across the full spectrum of modern industries, and will only become more so as technology and communications tools continue to evolve going forward.

II. INNOVATION IS EASIER THAN YOU THINK

Who says innovation has to be difficult when you apply a *FASTER* and more forward-thinking mindset? While game-changing breakthrough technologies and new scientific discoveries tend to hog media headlines, it bears remembering: Evolutionary changes (slight shifts in business strategy or thinking) can often be every bit as powerful as revolutionary advancements when it comes to successfully growing your business. All too often, at the pace today's market moves, and scale on which market leaders operate, we often forget — all it frequently takes for organizations to get ahead is just a minor shift in tactics or perspective. For example:

When L&T General Insurance — a full-service health, property, and casualty insurance provider — wanted to find a way to serve the hugely-diverse and hugely-scattered Indian market? Instead of applying a Western business model and attempting to install branches in every remote town and village and hoping customers would come to it, the company took a contrarian approach. Rather than leverage traditional market strategies, it flipped them on their heads, equipping insurance agents with smartphones and tablets on which a suite of online, cloud-based apps capable of issuing policies and processing claims on the spot was pre-installed, so that agents could go to customers instead. In less than 2 years, it built a $28,000,000 million business that had issued over 100,000 policies.

When medical device leader Medtronic wanted to expand its already successful business throughout Western Europe and beyond? It didn't double-down on cutting-edge devices. It reinvented its business model instead, expanding its offerings to include services, and establishing new business units that partnered to put owned-and-operated labs inside hospitals. Not only has Medtronic increased its business and provided partners with significant improvements in customer service and cost-savings by doing so. Having earned their trust, it's also built a sizable business around ancillary services such as supply chain management and performance benchmarking.

When French telecom giant Orange wanted to double the size of its innovation initiatives, but didn't want to invest millions in R&D or hordes of high-priced working professionals? It decided to outsource the entire process, and offered APIs — plug-and-play back-end software solutions — both to internal employees and external developers so that they could create new uses for Orange's technologies. Using just one of these solutions, the company was able to seamlessly integrate social and second-screen experiences from hundreds of film and TV companies into many of its services in under a year.

When Newell Rubbermaid's Contigo brand wanted to find a way to differentiate its products in the hugely-crowded and -contested market for portable containers and cups? It didn't invest a fortune into dozens of abortive product roll-outs, attempting to guess what working professionals on the go would want. It simply studied today's busiest travel sites, where commuters tended to congregate and — after discovering that passengers were constantly wiping off their mugs' mouth guards on napkins, sleeves, and handkerchiefs — it introduced a new line of travel mugs with special covers designed to keep out dirt.

And when MasterCard needed a new idea for a mobile payment app? It simply put the call out to employees at Innovation Express, a global series of hackathon events where business people, designers, and software developers team up to create new business plans and products in record time. Two days later, Qkr — which can let you order food from your seat at a stadium, or pre-order school lunches for children right from your pocket without ever setting foot in a cafeteria — was born.

>>>>ASK YOURSELF: WHAT KINDS OF INNOVATIVE NEW SOLUTIONS COULD YOUR ORGANIZATION PRODUCE IF YOU MADE EVEN THE SIMPLEST CHANGES?>>>>

As a modern executive, ask yourself: What kinds of innovative new solutions could your organization produce if you made even the simplest changes to the way in which you approached new product development? And just how powerful could simple shifts in positioning and messaging be in terms of helping you turbo-charge public outreach efforts by better fine-tuning them to connect with different audiences, or giving them a fresh shot of excitement and relevance? While it's not always obvious to the casual observer, innovation is far easier than you think. All it takes to successfully steer around a challenge, or overcome a problem, is simply a greater sense of perspective, and greater willingness to be more creative with how you apply the tools at-hand.

III. HOW TO TURBO-CHARGE CREATIVITY & GROWTH

So much for the status quo: Continuous change is the new normal and uncertainty the only certain in business today. To succeed in such disruptive times, organizations must growingly adopt a mindset that prioritizes speed and versatility alongside a more flexible business strategy. If you want to move *FASTER* – and create a self-sustainable way to drive growth and innovation – consider: Going forward, a *zero-based* (ZBx) approach to leadership and budgeting will be increasingly crucial to apply for enterprises hoping to get ahead in tomorrow's business environment. Businesses operating under this model will continuously reassess programs and processes to weigh their profitability and strategic relevance, and consistently reallocate resources from those initiatives that are underperforming to better-performing initiatives that support more rapid and pronounced business growth. "Forget about the past," says Kris Timmermans, senior managing director of supply chain, operations, and sustainability strategy for Accenture. "Agility is about better positioning yourself to succeed in a forward-thinking, disruptive world. If you properly plan and look to the future, you'll be better equipped to look to the future – and historic, past-looking budgets will only slow you down." Putting a focus on competitive agility, ZBx-based thinking helps businesses create a culture of innovation, allowing them to achieve startup-like speeds at enterprise-level scale – and more effectively compete in the face of ongoing transformation.

Wondering what it takes to create a similar mentality in your enterprise – and a culture that prizes routinely tying efforts and resources to results? You're not alone. In fact, according to Accenture, 80% of the G2000 are involved in enterprise-wide cost optimization efforts. But just 17% of CFOs believe their companies are properly organized to make the most of working capital, effectively build out future capabilities, and continue to develop competitive advantages.

Luckily, says Timmermans, shifting to a ZBx mindset doesn't have to be time-consuming or difficult. But it does require executives to champion a corporate culture where accountability and ownership are prized as much as actual hands-on accounting. "ZBx is about applying more practical thinking, and greater forethought – making sure you're more flexible, and continually linking efforts to positive outcomes while consistently reinvesting in growth-oriented initiatives and expanding your capabilities."

To thrive, a ZBx mentality – which views change as a constant, ongoing series of transformational activities that steadily expand an organization's comfort zone and capabilities – must first be embraced at the highest level. This requires a commitment from the CEO and leadership team to focus less on cost-cutting and more on the continuous reallocation of resources across the organization to maximize productivity and innovation. In particular, rather than projecting resource needs based on past demands (which often don't account for transformational changes and technologies impacting the business), leaders must adopt a mindset that favors future-focused growth. "By emphasizing accountability on top of cost ownership, and leveraging data-driven insights, organizations can quickly pivot and double down on more of what's working," explains Timmermans. "ZBx shifts the focus from pure cost-costing to linking efforts with outcome, and continuously reinvesting in creating competitive advantage and greater corporate agility."

For example, picture a consumer products company whose leadership team allocates budget towards a series of new products. Backed by analytics, each initiative is designed to help the company gain real-time insight into the nature of fast-changing markets. Using ZBx-based thinking, results are monitored to see which solutions are actually connecting with customers, incrementally improve products/services/solutions and surrounding communications efforts, or pivot to more successful strategies. By implementing this method of incremental advancement, and surrounding financial strategies, not only can the organization more forward *FASTER* and more intelligently – a system of ongoing growth and sustainable innovation is also achieved.

Likewise, to remain competitive, companies also need full visibility into organization-wide spending, so as to consistently reallocate funds that aren't being applied to successful ventures to those that promote tangible growth. This requires enterprise leaders to focus on four key areas of improvement – zero-based spend, organization, front office, and supply chain – in order to find the capital that's required to reinvest in growing their firm's capabilities and insights.

***

>> >> ZERO-BASED THINKING IS ABOUT STARTING WITH NOTHING AND JUSTIFYING EACH INVESTMENT YOU MAKE>> >>

***

Put simply:

• **Zero-Based Spend** allows organizations to determine where they're spending discretionary funds on expenses that aren't sunk labor costs to free up working capital. This allows corporate leaders to gain deeper insight into where these funds can be better allocated to promote business growth, boost productivity, and positively impact organizational culture. Rather than look in the rear-view mirror at last year's expenses, zero-based spend asks you to reconsider costs based on current needs – and where you may be able to free up working capital. Funds and resources can then be better redeployed to most quickly and effectively fuel growth and innovation. Asking a simple question – *Do more cost-effective and -efficient ways exist to achieve better results?* – can routinely produce huge windfalls. "In traditional budgeting, the standard is to look at last year's budget and anticipate marginal growth based on it," says Timmermans. "Using ZBx thinking, companies truly need to imagine that this figure is zero – and then justify each expense going forward."

• **Zero-Based Organization** is a logistical principle that allows you to streamline operations by reassigning talent from low-impact to high-priority initiatives that provide maximum benefit to the enterprise. To succeed, companies need to not only use technology to fuel growth at scale and automate repetitive or manual tasks that humans don't need to perform. They also need to better leverage human capital to make sure workers' efforts are rightsized, properly organized, and that the correct individuals are aligned with projects that best suit them and properly incentivized to focus on truly rewarding and value-creating work. To improve productivity and response times while becoming more flexible and agile, it's vital to most effectively align workers' efforts with areas of growth and profitability for the business. Zero-based organization lets you start from scratch by shifting talent away from work that doesn't contribute to desired outcomes to areas that leverage their unique skills to fuel growth and innovation while improving employee engagement.

• **Zero-Based Front Office** is a mindset that promotes the optimization of marketing, sales, and customer service efforts in order to lower customer acquisition costs while increasing customer spending. Examples include the use of customer relationship management (CRM) software, behavior monitoring tools, and predictive technologies to enhance the process of client outreach, and overall user experience. Using supporting methodologies and technologies, e.g. analytics, predictive insights, and CRM tools, you can better anticipate customer needs and lower acquisition costs while improving the overall user experience. "It's about streamlining, eliminating distractions, and improving cost savings," suggest Timmermans.

• **Zero-Based Supply Chain** provides the lens through which companies can re-examine their supply chain from the axis of three key variables – price, performance, and value engineering. This approach can help boost speed and maximize productivity while quickly slashing expenses by up to 5 – 10%. Rather than chase incremental cost savings, leaders use forensic insights and analytics to gain deeper visibility into organizational performance, in order to determine which strategic levers can be pulled to slash expenditures and boost output. For example, beverage leader AB InBev discovered that going 100%

renewable could dive huge cost savings on a running basis while also building ongoing goodwill with the public and doing good for the planet. Letting you reconsider your current business strategy from several angles (price, performance, and value engineering), a zero-based supply chain methodology lets you track every cost, and determine where exponential savings and performance gains can be recognized in record time.

Bear in mind: Traditional management strategies typically emphasize cost-cutting. But short-term gains often come at the expense of an organization's long-term health, and ability to compete. To get ahead in highly disruptive marketplaces, it's instead vital to instill a sense of transparency across the organization and create a culture that champions innovation, optimization, and smart decision-making. Rather than focus simply on curtailing spending, this means having to consistently reinvest in new initiatives that best support your organization's vision and bottom line over an extended horizon. Adopting a zero-based thinking model – wherein expenses are routinely monitored, and resources continually reallocated to most effectively optimize enterprise operations, output, and growth – can not only help you consistently find the capital to do so. When you make it a cornerstone of your leadership strategy, it can also help you instill a sense of ownership, entrepreneurship, and accountability in employees that serves as a vital source of growth, learning, and competitive advantage going forward.

"Zero-based thinking isn't just about budgeting (just one of many important steps to becoming more agile and achieving sustainable competitive advantages) though," explains Timmermans. "It's about starting with nothing and justifying each investment you make – then routinely considering how to reinvest funds and manpower strategically over time so that your organization can continuously get the maximum benefit from all of its investments."

HOW TO HARDWIRE ZBX THINKING INTO YOUR COMPANY CULTURE

Also important to note when it comes to driving sustainable growth and innovation: Like a crash diet, most cost-optimization efforts don't last – studies show that only 36% of companies surveyed agree that their business sustains the benefit of cost-optimization progress. In contrast, ZBx-based thinking offers a practical way to consistently manage costs on an ongoing, continuous basis, allowing you to discover new ways to smartly invest in your organization's future.

But to operationalize ZBx requires not only ownership by the CEO and senior leadership. It also requires these same leaders to instill a passion for change in their workforce, and find ways to empower intrepreneurs (entrepreneurial thinkers inside the organization) at every level, from providing greater organizational transparency to implementing platforms and tools for measuring and monitoring organizational effectiveness.

In the end, creating sustainable growth requires organizations to think *FASTER*, and invest in future-focused opportunities and technologies. Capable of being applied across every facet of an enterprise, zero-based thinking holds the potential to free up countless resources and reserves. These resources can quickly be reinvested into tomorrow's leaders and solutions, as well as building sustainable areas of growth.

Giving organizations of every size all the tools and insights that they need to adapt to shifting trends and stay ahead of changing markets, industry leaders in every field are increasingly embracing ZBx principles. New ways of doing business require new ways of thinking. Make the shift to a zero-based mindset, and you'll find your organization's prospects soaring to new heights as well. ZBx not only provides a readymade framework for doing so, it also provides a self-sustaining system for driving ongoing innovation in any business. "ZBx isn't just about leveraging strategic shifts that can help you make more money," says Timmermans. "It's about making your money work harder for you."

IV. HOW TO ENCOURAGE SUCCESSFUL INNOVATION

Surprise: Just when you think you've got any given industry mastered, that's when the next disruption hits. In fact, the single biggest theme in today's high-tech business world is unpredictability, according to PWC's CEO Survey. Worse, executives' say that their confidence in their enterprises' ability to grow is at an all-time record low. So how can your organization thrive in an age where senior leaders say that (even after years of investing in digital transformation) they're still hard-pressed to gain the insights needed to make smart decisions? Happily, the answers are simpler than you suspect.

As interviews with scores of industry-leading firms reveal, the secret to succeeding in uncertain times is simple. If you can't predict the future, start taking more risks, not fewer, and steadily investing in initiatives that drive ongoing learning and growth for your workforce instead. Likewise, they advise, since customers are repeatedly proven to be the business world's best, most reliable source of successful new ideas? It's imperative to more proactively put systems and solutions in place that can help frontline employees better monitor shoppers' shifting needs, and more rapidly and continuously adapt business strategies based on their feedback. In uncertain times, tech industry pros reveal, you've got to take more chances to get ahead in business. However, these risks should come in the form of smart, cost-effective bets on new initiatives (e.g. new product solutions or customer outreach campaigns) that can help you quickly gain deeper insights into changing customer preferences – and make more informed strategic choices in turn.

For example, for 65 years, Elmer's Products had been creating cutting-edge glues and adhesives under the direction of individual executives, who decided which products to make and when. But recently, the market began changing so fast that the company needed to get much faster about inventing new ideas to appeal to younger audiences, especially Millennials, more of whom were becoming parents. So Elmer's not only created a website where employees could speak up and suggest innovative new concepts. It built an internal team that was charged with getting workers to share their ideas more readily, and putting out open calls for ideas to partners, vendors, and even the general public. Thousands of submissions later, Elmer's is cranking out more successful concepts faster than ever. In fact, its cutting-edge School Glue Naturals line – created in partnership with a supplier, who helped invent the idea – is one of the first and most successful natural products of its kind to appear in classrooms nationwide.

***

>>>> WORTH REMEMBERING: MOST HIGH-TECH ORGANIZATIONS CAN NOW GO FROM CONCEPT TO EXECUTION WITH NEW IDEAS IN RECORD TIME>>>>

***

Worth remembering: Most high-tech organizations can now go from concept to execution with new ideas in record time. Likewise, our consulting firm has multibillion-dollar clients that are rolling out new apps every 6 weeks for $20,000 apiece all year round – just for the learning experiences these efforts provide. So if this is now your market reality, and you want to get better at operating in a world where customer needs and competitive landscapes are continually shifting? Not only is it high time to start challenging yourselves and your people to regularly think differently. You've also got to start putting communications tools in place that give workers the ability to help great ideas bubble from the bottom up, not just top down. And, for that matter, the freedom and flexibility to quickly adapt their business strategies to keep up with changing tastes.

In fact, the trick to succeeding in disruptive environs isn't difficult. You've simply got to constantly encourage your people to try new things; apply fresh strategies and solutions; track results; and learn from each venture, adapting your approaches to get better based on market feedback with each successive effort. (Steadily increasing odds of success along the way.) But it's important to also note: In order to do so, you also have to make a point to actively promote entrepreneurial thinking throughout the organization – and continuously give people room to focus on long-term as well as short-term goals by providing them with the tools, time, freedom, and support that they need to constantly tinker with and reimagine everything.

Happily, the ability to innovate your way to success is often far more accessible and affordable than you may think. You've merely got to make a point to routinely review the impact of your company's initiatives, and reallocate funds being poured into less well-performing initiatives into those best poised to make a real impact. Likewise, as a business leader, it's vital to move your organization's focus away strictly from one of strictly short-term cost-cutting to a focus on steadily reinvesting in long-term growth.

In effect, finding ways to stay relevant – and stay ahead of the curve – is easy when you're willing to keep an open mind and encourage your people to be more persistent when it comes to applying new approaches and strategies. *Forget the phrase "thinking outside of the box:" If you're thinking right, there are no boxes in place to begin with.* If you want to succeed in environments of constant disruption, and give people the tools they need to be more creative though? You've got to actively open yourself to a mentality that embraces change and reinvention – and that prizes creative thinking and new ways of doing business. The more you adopt a *FASTER*, more forward-thinking mindset, the more readily you'll be able to sustain upward growth, the more consistently you'll be able to stay competitive, and the more the future will always be what you choose to make of it, whatever tomorrow may bring.

V. HOW TO CREATE
LONG-TERM BUSINESS GROWTH

Contrary to popular belief, as we touched on prior, enterprises seeking to innovate and achieve sustainable growth need to do more than simply cut costs. As industry leaders in every field are increasingly becoming aware, it's also crucial to adopt a way of thinking which prizes ongoing learning and reinvestment. Per earlier chapters, top-down approaches to budgeting and one-off cost-saving exercises can provide temporary gains, but often cause firms to inadvertently excise potential sources of competitive advantage. Rather than simply slash expenses, tomorrow's most successful businesses instead routinely reassess strategic processes' and programs' value, then regularly reallocate savings gained from sidelining less productive ventures into activities that drive continued organizational learning and growth.

In today's marketplace, change and disruption are occurring at an unprecedented pace. With growth a top priority for organizations of every size, forward-thinking executives know that finding sustainable ways to streamline operations, pioneer winning solutions, and boost enterprises' marketability are vital to staying competitive. But an emphasis on pinching pennies alone often leads enterprises to kill promising new innovations, technologies, and solutions while still in the cradle. Worse, it frequently causes a company to abandon emerging areas of business or ignore changing customer needs in favor of pursuing other, more familiar initiatives with less growth potential. All can cripple an enterprise's ability to expand its capabilities, comfort zones, and insights, and cause executive leaders to prioritize short-term (and typically short-lived) gains over those activities that actually fuel long-term growth.

As modern-day thinking instead reminds us, to stay ahead of changing customer needs, and competitors, it isn't simply enough to operate more efficiently anymore. It's also vital to know where to double down and invest in pursuits that can boost your enterprise's agility and resilience. By regularly reevaluating expenses while also looking holistically across the organization and staying focused on the big picture, you can not only ensure every dollar is best spent. You can also more effectively bring your workforce's full range of insights and capabilities to bear, and guarantee that time, effort, and resources are most productively applied through the organization.

Rather than assume historical models will hold up in the face of ongoing disruption, contemporary approaches to budgeting instead force executive leaders to focus on what's happening here and now –

and give colleagues the tools that they need to help drive the business forward. Using models such as zero-based thinking (described in greater depth in preceding sections), executive leaders can essentially begin with a zero base and work to justify the need and cost for every line item, gaining deeper insights into how to maximize efficiency and sales revenues as part of the process. But more importantly, frameworks such as these provide the tools needed to optimize processes and procedures, boost organizational agility, and heighten flexibility in the face of shifting market demand. Helping lay the building blocks for future-proofing an enterprise, these solutions make it possible to create a more efficient operating model, build cutting-edge capabilities, and promote a culture of excellence throughout any given organization.

Moreover, myriad companies aren't just recognizing immediate cost savings by adopting such forward-thinking business models. They're also helping fuel sustainable growth in the form of international expansion, added brand-building activities, and the creation of innovative new products and services. For example, a global food company who partnered with a leading management consulting firm to double down on strategies that were working was able to implement a global supply chain, finance, human resources, and IT management platform that – while it came with greater short-term expenses attached – will save the firm $100 million on a recurring basis. Original equipment manufacturers (OEMs) are also using these types of operating approaches to optimize marketing strategies and inventory management models, e.g. a large electronic control board manufacturer who stopped hiring fleets of analysts to monitor market shifts and now uses computerized models to determine retail prices for its goods.

In fact, companies who leverage these types of innovation and budgeting strategies are seeing average cost reductions of 15% and bottom line savings of over $260 million annually, according to research by top analysts. Studies further show that more than 91% of these types of zero-based programs have met or exceeded their targets. Small wonder then that the category has grown a whopping 57% every year since 2013, underscoring its importance as an invaluable leadership tool that allows organizations to better allocate resources and align strategic priorities to drive winning results. And zero-based thinking (and budgeting) can be applied to nearly every facet of an organization, with savings frequently redirectable into high-priority areas such as growth initiatives, digital programs, acquisitions, research and development, and bottom-line expansion.

Businesses looking to empower their people and more readily funnel efforts and resources that don't support business growth into initiatives that do will find that closed-loop cost management strategies such as these provide a ready vehicle for growth. Helping you not only find significant savings, but also smartly reinvest them in the enterprise, closed-loop cost management approaches provide full visibility on all operating expenditures, and how you can more strategically leverage available resources to grow your business. Three essential components – transparency, accountability, and agility – can help you reduce overhead while building the finance and procurement capabilities you need to drive competitive advantage and sustain affordable long-term growth.

- **Transparency** provides a holistic view into all expenditures, so you can quickly see what was spent, where, and by whom – and identify opportunities to boost efficiency or cost savings. Armed with this information, zero-based budgeting allows you to strip away unnecessary expenditures, create detailed forecasts, and more effectively assign resources to those activities that heighten business growth.

- **Accountability** promotes greater cost-consciousness and compliance throughout the organization and creates a system that enables more effective resource consumption, as well as greater ability to monitor and adjust outgoing expenses. In effect, workers who adopt this principle begin to treat the company's money as their own and make smarter decisions that work towards the greater long-term good of the enterprise.

- **Agility** helps embed the idea of sustainable growth into the firm's cultural DNA. Not only does it champion the concept of regularly questioning the value of expenditures, and the need for ongoing change and transformation amongst employees. Challenging old ways of thinking, it also inspires organizations to ask themselves the question *"Is the way we've 'always done things' still the best way to do them?"* – noting that in today's fast-moving and hugely-volatile business world, the answer is typically no.

A simple, six-step methodology (which goes far beyond simple cost-cutting measures) can help you close the loop on cost-management, and champion zero-based and innovation-minded thinking throughout the organization, say leading experts:

- **Visibility** – Providing transparency on all expenditures through transaction data analysis.

- **Value Targeting** – Defining expense policies and procurement initiatives to reduce both price and consumption.

- **Category Ownership** – Creating an accountability matrix to promote ownership of every expense.

- **Zero-Based Budgeting** – Starting with a budget of zero every year so as to help you detect and eradicate unnecessary expenses.

- **Procurement Execution** – Securing price reductions with suppliers by executing strategic buying and sourcing operations.

- **Control and Monitoring** – Conducting monthly reviews to identify budget variances and action plans to address them.

Adaptable to virtually any business, or business challenge, market leaders in a myriad of sectors are using these types of forward-thinking strategic methods to generate breakthrough results.

For example, telecom is just one of many areas of business being revolutionized by ZBx enterprises. Facing increasing pressure from new technologies and digital upstarts, communications service providers (CSPs) are increasingly looking for ways to free up funds to adapt to market shifts and compete with often smaller, more nimble challengers. To fuel continued growth, many aren't simply switching to a zero-based budgeting model, in which organizations start from zero to determine which line items should be reduced and resources funneled into more productive efforts. They're also increasingly adopting a ZBx mindset – one wherein resources are continually optimized, and operations streamlined – to improve workforce and supply chain management needs as well as help reduce overhead costs. Doing so doesn't just allow established CSPs to recognize immediate savings by eliminating non-working money from their budgets. It also allows these enterprises to more quickly and cost-effectively deploy talent and resources, as well as roll out new initiatives ranging from automation to artificial intelligence, analytics, and machine learning technology that help lay the groundwork for future growth.

>>>>MARKET LEADERS IN NUMEROUS SECTORS ARE USING FORWARD-THINKING STRATEGIC METHODS TO GENERATE BREAKTHROUGH RESULTS>>>>

To put things in comparison: Leading consulting and strategy providers find that traditional cost reduction strategies are only capable of achieving 35% of the savings that the Top 50 CSPs need to ensure ongoing category leadership. By way of contrast, implementing ZBx thinking has allowed one major CSP to eliminate a whopping 20% of its entire total annual expenses by rethinking all network-related operating expenses from the ground up instead – potentially saving it billions. Another CSP applied zero-based principles and eliminated $550 million in yearly expenses as well. With customer acquisition/retention efforts and general overhead additionally representing around a fifth of many CSP's standard annual operating expenses, it's also worth noting. The use of ZBx-based programs and supporting technologies such as machine learning and robotic process automation (RPA) can produce massive savings and improvement of margins across the board in other areas of business as well.

Myriad sectors such as finance and banking are also primed for revolutionary change in coming years. The rise of Millennial and Gen Z audiences, growing global redistribution of wealth, and rapidly-shifting customer habits are quickly transforming the commercial landscape. Digital disruption further threatens to upend traditional business models in these industries, even as market leaders' regulatory demands and compliance needs continue to skyrocket as well. Zero-based tools and strategies offer a solution for adapting to these unprecedented changes.

By way of illustration, tomorrow's marketplace belongs to digitally native banks, as a number of top management consulting firms note, which will interact seamlessly with clients across a range of channels, including mobile and online mediums. To succeed in such fast-moving and unpredictable environments, firms are growingly leveraging ZBx-based solutions to monitor and predict audience needs, automate operations, and remain a trusted presence at every touchpoint in which they interact with end-users. Future-ready banks are also working to extensively integrate zero-based thinking across every facet of their operations in order to stay agile and flexible enough to respond to emerging opportunities and challenges.

The complexity, cost, and scale needed to complete the transformation journey to a future-proof organization and find the resources required to power such transitions are staggering, according to recent business research. To successfully navigate these shifts, finance and banking leaders are having to adopt new ways of thinking. Zero-based methodologies and solutions provide an affordable, turnkey way to drive ongoing growth – and achieve far greater savings than typical cost reduction strategies. Encouraging firms to adopt closed-loop approaches to accounting (wherein every expense is challenged and justified), apply new digital tools to improve the customer journey, and find more efficient ways to operate, ZBx thinking provides fuel for innovation.

Switch to a mindset and operating model that embraces these concepts, and no matter your field of expertise, you can empower your organization to move FASTER – and ensure that it's more future-ready. Likewise, doing so can also help you embed a greater sense of purpose into the enterprise. But most importantly, embracing a ZBx mindset allows you to create a self-sustaining engine for growth that can help you protect core business lines while pioneering fresh and innovative ways to engage tomorrow's audience.

As a result, leaders in every field are applying zero-based mindsets and strategies' core principles to become more resilient and innovative. In the oil and gas sector, where economic downturns are commonplace and prices prone to rapid decline, providers are leveraging ZBx approaches to weather these downturns and make the most of upswings. In the healthcare industry, providers are capitalizing on these tools to deliver more cost-effective and convenient services to patients, while leading manufacturers, retailers, and distributors are utilizing such solutions to better manage demand and supply chain operations. But future applications for ZBx principles are endless, from rightsizing consumer products development and marketing efforts to finding more cost-efficient ways to manage global workforces and fleets of vehicles or field service technicians. No matter the industry or size of the organization, zero-based tools and solutions offer a better way to approach business management.

To ensure a brighter future for your organization tomorrow, start planting seeds of change today. Rather than simply focus on cost-cutting, take a smarter look at where efforts and expenses can be reduced, and reapplied to more rapidly create positive change and impact the bottom-line. Adopting a zero-based mindset not only allows you to identify massive opportunities for cost savings. It also helps provide the essential resources and insights you need to drive continued learning, future-proof your enterprise, and build a self-sustaining system for achieving long-term growth.

Clearly, at odds with popular thinking, simply cutting costs is not a recipe for business success, let alone one for driving long-term and sustainable growth. Instead, today's most accomplished enterprises recognize that savings gained from expense-trimming exercises must be regularly and smartly reinvested back into the organization to fuel ongoing expansion. By routinely reassessing a firm's expenditures, and continually optimizing the allocation and use of its resources – including resources such as human capital and top performers – forward-thinking enterprises don't just gain the tools they need to drive huge market wins. They also gain all the insights and capabilities that they need to regularly build and rewrite the blueprint for tomorrow's success.

VI. WHY INCENTIVIZATION IS THE NEW INNOVATION

As a futurist and trends expert, I attend numerous conferences on how to create positive change and accelerate business growth each year. Ironically, executives might be surprised to note that the number one buzzword as of late at these events isn't actually *innovation* anymore. Rather, with studies consistently showing that end-users (i.e. everyday shoppers) are today's most reliable source of winning new ideas, and frontline workers (those closest to them) are typically the most informed audience in any organization? The big buzzword these days is actually *incentivization* – a.k.a. how to motivate your workforce to routinely speak up, share their insights, and make more concerted attempts at rapidly transforming ideas into actionable solutions instead. Happily, finding ways to boost employee engagement, and your ability to spark positive change, doesn't have to be difficult. You can radically increase your ability to lead and succeed just by making a few simple adjustments in strategy and thinking to your leadership and workforce development strategies going forward.

***

>> >> *EVOLUTIONARY CHANGES CAN PROVE EVERY BIT AS POWERFUL AS REVOLUTIONARY CHANGES AT DRIVING POSITIVE BUSINESS RESULTS* >> >>

***

To begin with, it helps to realize that simple shifts in business or communication strategy – or even simple shifts in presentation or packaging – can prove every bit as powerful as breakthrough innovations at driving positive results. That's because in today's high-tech world, where one person or one idea can change the shape of an entire organization, *evolutionary* changes (minor tweaks in approach) can prove every bit as powerful as *revolutionary* changes, especially as they're more frequently implemented and compound over time. For example, a group of racquet clubs in the Midwest have sent their revenues soaring by installing high-tech courts that let players digitally track performance, analyze every swing, and compete against rivals on social scoreboards. Likewise, several category-leading sports providers across the Southwest boosted sign-ups 500% by introducing a "Sets in the City" program for 18- to 40-year-old tennis players that invited them to play in fun, fast-paced, and social leagues that paired play with visits to local happy hours and restaurants.

But in addition to reminding people how simple it is to create positive change at every turn when you apply simple shifts in thinking, you've also got to provide them with all sorts of welcome and inviting forums where they feel comfortable speaking up – and can make their voice heard. For example, one large government agency we work with has found ways to fast-track learning and growth by specifically adding positions for young professionals to contribute to on its internal committees, and holding regular meet-and-greets where experienced and emerging team leaders are encouraged to sit down, share fresh ideas, and collaborate in casual settings. Likewise, a popular non-profit association has found ways to unleash innovation at scale – and more rapidly identify emerging trends and topics of interest – by offering online matchmaking tools to members that allow them to quickly find and partner with researchers with similar interests in different fields. In effect, finding ways to win with innovation isn't just about implementing a variety of programs and platforms that allow for greater teamwork and communication. It's also about offering staffers more rapid ways to transform ideas into action, and creating more opportunities that allow them to consistently speak up, take ownership of challenges, and make necessary shifts in strategy when they see the need for change impending.

>>*PERFECTING CUSTOMER EXPERIENCE:*

BUILDING COMPETITIVE ADVANTAGE

I. HOW TO GET CRUCIAL CUSTOMER DATA

So much for pouring thousands into product testing labs and super-sized R&D teams. As businesses (and business leaders) are becoming increasingly aware, finding ways to better get to know your customers, and make more data-driven decisions, is a surer way to find success going forward. Following, you'll find several hints and tips that can help your business become both faster and far more effective at gathering and interpreting customer information – and translating insights into actionable strategy going forward.

1. Polls and Surveys – To truly get to know your customer, and gain the information that you need to make better data-driven decisions, it pays to invite them to contribute feedback and insights at every turn. Polls and surveys, which provide a level of visibility into customer satisfaction; how buyers perceive your products, services, and solutions; and how well any programs or campaigns are connecting with them, are an essential measurement tool here. Happily, a variety of free and paid apps, software plug-ins, and online services make it easy to build e-mail questionnaires, pop-up forms, and integrate interactive queries into either your website or online shopping system. Note: To get objective feedback as you go about polling end-users, be sure to ask smart, concise questions, one at a time, that are designed to keep answers specific and focused. If you'd like more open-ended feedback instead, you can always add separate questions to surveys at the end, as customer queries should always start simple before slowly ramping up in complexity. Likewise, when asking for customers' input, be sure to remember that it's important to (a) incentivize feedback with rewards (i.e. free downloads or discounts) (b) remind participants that their contributions are valued and (c) promptly respond and follow-up at every turn. The more shoppers feel you're listening and that you care, the more they'll share.

2. Product Trials and Tests – One of the best ways to gain additional customer information and feedback, and prompt rapid learning, iteration, and growth inside your business, is to invite customers to try products, services, and solutions in advance while they're still in development. Providing early product and service trials not only helps you see how well customers react to these solutions, but also gain deeper insights into how audiences are using them, and potential concerns that they may encounter. Oftentimes, these types of interactive, hands-on usability tests can surface opportunities or issues of interest that are hard to predict in advance, and can help make next steps to take from a strategic standpoint clearer for your business. Rapid prototyping also allows for rapid improvement and iteration, as user feedback and data-driven decisions can regularly help inform development, leading to enhanced product and service results. Early testers – who are often rewarded for their participation with additional perks and bonuses – won't just relish the opportunity to help you improve your business offerings either. They'll also provide you with detailed customer information and insights every step of the way. Such approaches can provide a highly-insightful and hugely cost-effective approach to focus group testing, and data gathering, that's hard to beat.

3. Crowdsourcing and Contests – Want to turbo-charge the amount of customer information coming in by several orders of magnitude? Try crowdsourcing contributions, a.k.a. putting out open calls to the general public. Whether asking shoppers to submit comments, suggestions, videos, photos, graphic designs, or other forms of content, many consumer-facing companies are finding success by running regular creative contests and democratizing the decision-making process. (Say by asking audiences for help when naming products or designing new ad campaigns.) Surprisingly, many of the world's top brands (and government agencies) are using these types of solutions to positive effect as well, including (a) hugely accelerating the pace and scale at which they can surface promising new ideas, topics, and trends for exploration (b) putting a more human face on their organization and (c) vastly multiplying the amount of feedback they're able to ingest, so they can make smarter data-driven decisions faster and more frequently.

4. Community Outreach – Even in an always-connected age where more and more interactions are going online and digital with each passing day, don't forget either: There's still no substitute for speaking directly with shoppers. If you want to truly get to know your customer, don't forget the importance of talking with them frequently, which is why so many businesses are now investing in community managers, as well as message boards, chat rooms, presences on social networks, and other dedicated online forums. Creating comfortable and inviting online spaces where customers are able to congregate, converse, and share insights and information can be among a modern business' most effective ways of sourcing crucial information. Likewise, it's also important for your business to serve as a thought leader within these spaces, and routinely prompt constructive discussion and debate around emerging topics of interest. The more robust your online presence, and more you interact with your user community, the more informed your business strategies and solutions will ultimately be.

5. Social Media – Think of social networks as the world's largest cocktail parties: Spaces where people like to gather, share ideas, and discuss the latest topics and trends. Accordingly, learning to be a better listener on these channels can help your organization more readily adapt to changing times and trends, and even predict customer needs before customers themselves are aware of them. Not only do social channels provide a helpful resource through which to gather candid input from shoppers by reviewing comments, conversations, and interactions. You can also glean helpful insights by monitoring the tone of these interactions, and which topics are trending, that can help shape any business plan for the better. A wise organization not only makes a point to participate on social networks, but also invest in tools for staying attuned to which subjects are trending online – and what people have to have to say about them.

From leveraging analytics tools that can reveal how much time people are spending on your website (and where they're spending it) to holding regular meetings with your customer service and tech support teams, there are many high- and low-tech ways to get to know your customer better and faster. Happily, such solutions don't always have to be difficult or expensive to deploy. Today's organization has more tools and solutions for gathering customer information, and transforming data-driven decisions into hugely successful business results, available at its fingertips than ever. Better yet, these solutions can be implemented with less time and expense than ever before as well.

II. HOW TO BUILD BRAND LOYALTY

Customer retention has a simple definition: It describes an organization's ability to keep and retain customers. Implementing powerful customer retention strategies is key to success for any modern business. Given that it's 5X more expensive to attract a new customer than it is to keep a current one, and even just a 5% increase in customer retention rates is enough to potentially boost your company's profitability by 25-95%, according to Bain & Co., it's easy to see why. Coupled with the fact that seven in ten shoppers say that customer experience is important to purchasing decisions, yet less than half believe that companies provide good experiences today, the message for working professionals is clear. Investing in winning customer retention marketing campaigns and making a point to leverage the power of customer retention services should be a priority for any organization hoping to build and maintain competitive advantage going forward. Here, we'll discuss a number of new and novel ways you can boost customer retention rates more rapidly, increase shopper loyalty, and keep buyers coming back for more.

Strategy #1 – Provide clients with a little something extra.

Back in the 19th century, tradespeople and shopkeepers in New Orleans used to give a free bonus – a lagniappe (pronounced: lanny-yap), as they called it – to favorite customers as a token of appreciation. Given that everyone loves surprise gifts, and the amount of goodwill that they can engender, ask yourself: What unexpected extras could you provide existing clients that would surprise and delight them in extra measure (and help build similar brand loyalty) today as well? Happily, in the high-tech era, there are a variety of cost-affordable options you can offer in addition to physical goods, or traditional discounts and rebates. For example: Providing customers with free upgrades on service or software packages; complementary digital copies of your company's latest book or research report; no-cost access to exclusive online events and seminars featuring special brand-name guests; or digital credits that they can redeem for virtual goods of every kind. Keeping in mind that shoppers are used to only getting what they pay for, offering an added bonus without prompting is often a great way to help enhance your relationship and drive repeat purchases.

Strategy #2: Target shoppers with personalized offers.

The more you get to know your customer, the more effective at crafting individualized messaging and offers that are designed to catch their interest that you'll be. Luckily, myriad high-tech analytics tools now let you track shoppers' online behavior, and each action that they take when interacting with your brand, so that you can provide more informed responses every step of the way. Among today's most effective forms of customer retention marketing, contextualized promotions – which provide personalized discounts, specials, and offers at the moment customers are most receptive to them – can be a powerful asset in your promotional toolbox. Whether they take the form of contextual prompts (which recognize recent purchases or call-ins by the customer); chat bots (artificially intelligent personalities that can converse like humans) combined with customer relationship management (CRM) tools that recognize why shoppers may be reaching out; or location-based offers (which pop-up when someone nears your business or a competing outlet), there are many ways to put customer retention services to work in your favor.

Strategy #3: Incentivize social engagement and sharing.

Many businesses survive and thrive based on the goodwill and enthusiasm of their fans, who often look to social networks, video sharing sites, and similar multimedia aggregators for insights and inspiration when making buying decisions. So if you want to improve customer retention marketing efforts, and boost online engagement rates, why not turn around and put the spotlight on your community? Incentivizing user-generated content – e.g. video clips and selfies – featuring your products, services, or solutions can be a powerful way to help drive awareness, increase brand reach, and drive social media engagement. Naturally, you can reward active customers for doing so with freebies, points redeemable for prizes, and/or other special perks. By encouraging community members to spread the word, and helping readers/viewers keep your products, services, or solutions top of mind, you can create a compelling and authentic way to build awareness.

Strategy #4: Offer flexible perks that cater to shoppers' interests.

Many businesses reward loyalty members with points for performing a variety of different activities – e.g. purchasing products, liking their social network channels, downloading official apps, etc. But more often than not, these points are redeemable for one thing and one thing only: Whatever goods you're currently stocking. However, the best customer retention strategies instead speak to shoppers' interests, and offer a wider variety of rewards tailored to buyers' lifestyles. For example, if you're an outdoor apparel retailer, you might offer shoppers all manner of adventurous travel experiences and vacations, or if you're a food service provider, you might offer them access to a number of cooking classes or invites to unique dinner events. The key is to create curated rewards that better speak to your target audience, rather than offering generic, one-size-fits-all solutions – i.e. 10% discount offers. No matter whether you're running an architecture firm or craft beer distributor, there are many ways to create loyalty and reward programs designed with your specific target consumer in mind.

Strategy #5: Pay it forward and spread goodwill.

Today's customer is more socially conscious than ever. Moreover, they much prefer to do business with organizations that are in the business of doing good as well. So if you're looking to enhance customer retention rates, consider implementing a loyalty program that can help truly make a difference by supporting a host of good causes on a global scale. For example: Rather than give customers cash back on purchases, you might instead funnel a portion of every purchase to fund worthy causes, or give shoppers the option to donate funds to their pick of several charities. Finding better ways to appeal to customers' values and design loyalty programs that help them actively achieve their goal of creating positive change in the world isn't just a positive thing to do. It's also just one of many simple, innovative customer retention strategies that you can start implementing today that can help you boost audience goodwill, even as you boost your company's fortunes as well.

Strategy #6: Use success stories to get the message across.

These days, it's no secret that effective storytelling is one of the best forms of marketing available to businesses today. Keeping this in mind, significant portions of your customer retention and sales outreach efforts should be focused on sharing case studies and examples of how clients are using your solutions to create positive results. Ask yourself: Are customers aware of all the many ways that your offerings can help them – and are they using these solutions and all their features to best effect? Wherever possible, take the time to educate them about the benefits and upsides your business offers through the lens of success stories featuring organizations just like their own. The more you make a point to remind clients of the myriad ways you can assist them, and paint a practical picture of how to implement these partnerships in practice, the more repeat business you'll be poised to do. Peer validation can be a powerful tool for driving additional sales – and you know what they say about the squeaky wheel getting the grease.

III. HOW TO CONNECT WITH TOMORROW'S CUSTOMER

As rapidly as modern shopping environments are evolving, brands have to be far more agile and adaptable about shifting strategies to connect with today's customers and meet their quickly-changing needs. Luckily for business leaders, a newer, more flexible suite of secure technology and data insights solutions allows organizations to move *FASTER*, better plan around uncertainty, and engage shoppers across the full online, mobile, and retail buying spectrum.

"Growing access to the Internet of Things (IoT) and analytics tools allows market leaders to more effectively understand buyer preferences and behaviors, and strategize accordingly," explains Michael Colaneri, VP of Global Business – Retail Solutions for AT&T. "By tapping into a network of connected devices and apps which are constantly sharing information and talking to one another, retailers can better predict inventory needs, cut costs, and enhance the overall customer experience."

Using the tools that digital leaders provide, retailers can not only access scalable, turnkey solutions for enhancing supply chain operations, boosting workforce productivity, and improving consumer-facing communications. Backed by world-class insights and analytics, these solutions also allow forward-thinking organizations to predict when and where tomorrow's shoppers will be, what they'll be hunting for – and which messages they'll find most receptive.

On the back-end, says Colaneri, such advancements enable businesses to gain the ability to more effectively geo-target where retail outlets should be located, pre-anticipate staffing or inventory needs, and shrink order pick-up times from 30 minutes to under 150 seconds. On the front-end, he suggests, they allow organizations of every size – even those with online-only storefronts – to be able to better predict which products to stock, when to put them in front of shoppers, and how to best present these goods to potential buyers to maximize sales and conversion rates.

"Costs to acquire and retain customers (as well as fulfill orders) are growing, even as shoppers' expectations are skyrocketing and these individuals are becoming increasingly digitally proficient," Colaneri explains. "From automated tools to analytics programs, high-tech and IoT solutions are becoming increasingly crucial to have in-hand for retail leaders looking to stay ahead of the curve."

Allowing organizations to streamline operations, slash expenses, and better redeploy savings to focus on more quickly moving product out the door instead of simply managing inventory, such technology empowers market leaders to more rapidly deploy cutting-edge retail solutions. Capable of traveling everywhere that customers go – brick-and-mortar stores, online outlets, etc. – it also allows retail leaders to craft shopping experiences that are truly unique and different. Just a few examples include providing digital signage in stores that targets specific audiences, as well as individually-personalized deals, discounts, and brand promotions on their mobile devices when they drive nearby them.

"Letting you centralize operations and optimize customer outreach efforts, [these types of] solutions can help you increase sales and market share," says Colaneri. "But equally importantly, they provide a foundational network that lets you seamlessly connect every customer touchpoint across the shopping experience from mobile device to point of sale – and more effectively connect retail operations to revenue."

IV. HOW TECHNOLOGY IS TRANSFORMING HEALTHCARE

The future of healthcare is here, and we're pleased to report that it goes far beyond options to browse reviews of doctors online, or skim search engine activity to see what medical conditions are on the rise. What's more, thanks to the growingly ubiquitous availability of high-speed Internet connections, mobile devices, and other emerging technology trends (coupled with explosive growth in communications platforms), it looks to be much brighter for both tomorrow's providers and patients alike. Following, you'll find a sneak peek at five new high-tech healthcare trends that promise to rapidly transform the shape of the medical field going forward. And, for that matter, a number of shifts in market and business trends coming to the industry that organizations looking to capitalize on these upsides would do well to be aware of their wake.

5G Connectivity – Providing fiber-optic-like high-speed data transfers, and near instantaneous download and response times, 5G wireless network technology trends promise to utterly transform the shape of healthcare within the next two years. Potential applications for the technology, which enables larger and more sophisticated software programs to run without a hiccup on a wide range of mobile devices (even without having to be downloaded), are endless. Picture a world in which Malaysian surgeons will use robots to flawlessly operate on patients in Miami from thousands of miles away. Alternately, imagine one in which medical students from around the nation can come together over their cell phones to jointly perform instructor-led examinations right from their couch. Like the ability to instantly search online medical databases and cross-reference millions of test results on-demand, these are just two the many types of applications 5G high-speed networking enables. And that's before you factor in the many workforce applications it empowers, such as allowing hospitals and care facilities to juggle patients, manage medical inventories, market themselves, stay on top of customer relationships, and process paperwork far more effectively as well.

The Internet of Things (IoT) – Billions of devices are currently connected and communicating online, and unfathomable amounts of data now being generated every single day. Just a few new innovations and emerging business trends that all these advancements are powering: Pill bottles that can track when they're opened to make sure you're following your doctor's advice; DNA registers capable of gathering and analyzing information from millions of patients; and high-tech clothes and accessories that can collect and process detailed data on your everyday lifestyle and exercise habits. Coupled with growing digitization of medical testing and records, all are enabling much more in-depth and comparative health-related analyses to occur, and making it easier than ever to gauge the efficacy, impact, and risk of potential treatment options for different patients. In effect, the scale at which healthcare providers can now conduct surveys, cross-referencing ,and comparison is unrivaled – allowing for more in-depth testing and effective care than ever before.

Telemedicine – Over 3 billion people currently utilize a smartphone, with nearly 4 billion expected to be packing one by 2021, driving the growth of new healthcare trends. So it's no surprise that more providers are offering ways to research and interact with healthcare providers online or engage in audio- or video-conferencing sessions with medical professionals via various mobile devices on-demand. Whether you're looking to schedule a call with a nurse to get their advice on treating a head cold, or plan a video chat with your doctor to take a closer look at your sneezing symptoms? It's hard to argue with the time and money that such solutions can help save, especially since you can arrange for and engage in appointments from virtually anywhere you've got an Internet connection. Likewise, many areas of the developing world, e.g. India, are already taking advantage of a fast-growing range of downloadable apps that allow phone handsets to quickly transform into portable heart-rate monitors and other helpful tools as well. This level of convenience is increasingly helping to alleviate time and cost pressures on medical providers and patients, and bringing transformative capabilities to areas of the world that may otherwise struggle to receive adequate healthcare.

Wearable Devices – According to eMarketer, a quarter of all American adults (56.7 million people), will use a wearable device at least once a month every month today. Between smart watches, wrist-mounted trackers and Internet-connected clothes, many are collecting personalized, real-time data on health and fitness habits – data that's increasingly being used to inform medical research, enhance sleep habits, and improve well-being. From helping individuals' optimize eating and exercise plans to assisting them as they work to reduce stress and cultivate healthier behaviors, all promise to transform both the healthcare field (and public healthiness levels) going forward. Some insurance companies are even incentivizing customers to embrace a more active lifestyle by offering plan pricing discounts for customers who track their steps and make a point to exercise more – helping slash health-related risks and costs for all parties involved.

3D Printing – From prosthetics to standard-issue medical supplies, 3D printing – which allows you to create and make physical objects as needed – promises to upend the healthcare business, letting virtually anyone design and build custom solutions on-command. Moreover, a growing range of downloadable templates (aka digital blueprints) and thriving community of online creators is only helping innovative care options and ideas to spread further and faster. Researchers are already exploring futuristic applications and market trends such as the 3D printing of bone, muscle, and skin tissue as well. Who knows? Looking ahead, you may even be able to obtain custom-designed or -enhanced body parts.

Just a few additional healthcare-related trends and advancements you might expect to see enhancing customer experiences in the near future may also include:

• Open cloud healthcare innovation portals where manufacturers, software developers, service providers and more can source ideas (including from members of the general public) to help build tomorrow's solutions.

• Mobile innovations that let you quickly research, compare prices, and buy medical devices or source care-related services from a pool of private providers, all of whom are rated and recommended by users such as yourself.

• Websites where you can post advertisements for medical or healthcare-related needs, set your price, and sit back and watch industry professionals compete to bid on them.

• Wellness programs that let you connect, share data, and collaborate with other individuals in your city or neighborhood to help build positive fitness and health habits, and even enjoy discounts or rewards for making progress.

As you might imagine, these advancements may impact the healthcare industry in many ways, such as:

• Lowered barriers to entry, ushering in a wave of new solutions and providers, and producing heightened competition on pricing, service, and value.

• Increased ability on consumers' part to research and shop around for health- and care-related products and services.

• More data being shared online, and having to be managed, than ever before.

• Additional emphasis on the need for customer service, loyalty, and relationship-building – before, during, and after purchase decisions.

Noting this, while the future of the healthcare industry currently looks bright, it will look very different from today's field when it arrives. In addition, the changes it will bring will also create many opportunities and challenges for business operators. However, these shifts promise to usher in a new wave of innovation and advancement for the field: A wave that forward-thinking businesses who make a point to think *FASTER* and stay on top of changing market trends should be able to successfully ride for years to come.

V. IMPROVING THE INSURANCE EXPERIENCE

Digital disruption is everywhere in business today, but few industries are feeling its impact as much as the insurance business. Case in point: Nearly nine in ten carriers now agree that technology is advancing at an exponential rate – and that they must innovate exponentially to maintain a competitive edge as well. As a result, providers are increasingly turning to data-driven insights, analytics, and other high-tech tools to drive forward growth and make better decisions. Not only can these solutions greatly reduce risk, improve shopper satisfaction, and send profits soaring while shaving up to 30% of costs off incoming claims. Experts at McKinsey also note that they'll have a seismic impact on all aspects of the insurance industry going forward, from distribution to underwriting, pricing, and more.

"The future of insurance lies in leveraging technology and business intelligence to more effectively weigh opportunities, right-size risks, and predict customer needs," explains Gary Hallgren, president of pioneering telematics and data analytics provider Arity. "Insurance companies have always been good at collecting information, and were big data firms before the concept became popular... companies like ours, which analyze billions of insights from on-road driving behaviors to claims filings, are simply finding ways to help them utilize this information more effectively. For example: As we discovered in the automotive space, how you actually act behind the wheel is more important when assessing risks or offering competitively-priced/-packaged insurance policies than simply reviewing your credit score."

Unsurprisingly, providers in every field – including property & casualty, health, life, auto insurance, and more – are actively making significant investments in giving business operations a cutting-edge upgrade. With technology and digital-native customers currently reshaping every aspect of the insurance industry, it's no wonder that more than

600 "insurtech" companies have raised over $8.5 billion since 2014, with associated windfalls having doubled from 2017 to 2018 alone. "It's about being more connected with customers, and having the ability to better identify, quantify, and proactively predict what drives decision-making," says Hallgren. "Given how much we're already seeing such forward-thinking high-tech concepts transform the insurance industry, you can rest assured that top carriers are all eventually going to embrace similar models going forward."

Consider the future of transportation, for example. Today, over 240 million vehicles are used just 4% of the time in America, with 20-40% of cities' real estate devoted to parking, and 8 billion hours of citizens' lives currently wasted waiting in traffic. With ridesharing on the upswing, the number of licensed drivers on the decline, and auto sales shrinking, tomorrow's roads will inevitably play home to more single-purpose rentals, self-driving vehicles, and pay-as-you-go insurance plans. Thanks to insights from providers like Arity, given your current driving history, specific route to a destination, and even on-road traffic conditions, you'll soon be able to enjoy ultra-customized trip insurance plans on an as-needed and real-time basis. Likewise, should an accident happen while you're traveling, self-aware autos will be able to automatically assess damage, and you'll be able to submit claims and start inspection processes just by sending pictures from your smartphone.

Similar solutions also stand poised to revolutionize the process of obtaining and utilizing insurance policies in other fields as well. For example, when researching possible health or life insurance providers, artificially-intelligent systems will soon recognize your personal history, behaviors, and potential risk profile, and quickly customize and price offers for you in minutes. Likewise, underwriting for property and casualty insurance products will also become increasingly digitally automated, drawing upon multiple sources of data to provide optimal solutions in seconds. Self-aware computers so smart that they can pass for humans will further help you submit and process claims in coming years, and connected devices with built-in sensors will assess the extent of damage or loss associated with them. In short, from machine learning to robotics, a host of high-tech enhancements are currently working to make every aspect of the insurance business from picking a policy to processing submissions simpler, faster, and more cost-efficient.

"What we're currently seeing is a perfect storm of convergence in the industry, and technology is the enabler," suggests Jay Weintraub, co-founder and CEO of InsureTech Connect, the world's largest insurtech event. "Connectivity is now a fundamental aspect of consumers' everyday lives, and has changed the way in which they expect to interact and do business with brands of every kind – including insurance providers. With startups growingly leveraging cutting-edge technologies from machine learning to drones and digital automation to eliminate paperwork, speed up processing times, and more accurately process claims, things only get more interesting from here."

What's more, in addition to providing significant cost savings and process improvements, many leading companies are even using access to a growing range of high-tech tools to launch entirely new business models. As devices and digital records continue to become more connected and intertwined, expect to only see more upstart insurance carriers working to proactively identify new sales prospects, and tailor targeted solutions to fit them, say top market analysts. Along with this bustling business ecosystem will come even more robust hardware, software, and open-source tools, leading to even more rapid-fire advancements and opportunities for forward-thinking providers in the space as it continues to evolve.

"Looking ahead, it's not hard to envision how technology can help power more effective and engaging experiences for both individuals and businesses of every size," says Weintraub. "Thanks to new high-tech developments, the insurance industry is poised to see some big changes in coming years – changes that will only continue to help it evolve for the better."

VI. PICTURING TOMORROW'S WORLD OF FINANCE

Imagine using your credit card as a subway ticket, waving it at a movie poster to reserve seats, and splitting the cost of dinner with friends electronically on the fly. Tomorrow's most popular payment options will let you do just that. With credit card usage at an all-time high and 83% of Millennials (today's largest generation) now owning them, not only are such solutions quickly replacing cash as today's most convenient form of payment. Smarter and more self-aware, they're also undergoing a host of revolutionary high-tech upgrades that will make them even more of an all-purpose financial solution in the years ahead.

Forget standing in line at a ticket booth or grocery checkout line. In an age of cryptocurrencies, digital wallets, and mobile finance apps, you'll soon be able to wirelessly pay for anything, even monthly bills such as rent, on-demand right from the palm of your hand. Capable of acting as two-way transfer devices, tomorrow's cards will also enable cashless, peer-to-peer transactions, so you can transfer money easily amongst individuals when it's time to settle up a drinking or dining tab. Whether using sensors directly built into tomorrow's leading cards, or futuristic payment terminals housed at various retailers, security won't be a concern either. The world's largest financial firms are already working to build fingerprinting, facial/voice recognition, and other biometric technologies into cards to ensure everything's legit.

As the cost and size of digital storage continues to shrink, credit cards are increasingly becoming capable of storing information as well. All may soon function as forms of virtual ID, akin to drivers licenses, allowing us access to everything from our apartment doors to neighborhood gyms. Among the over 7 billion devices connected and communicating online, links to the Internet of Things won't just help providers to become smarter about offering audiences more personalized payment and credit options either. They'll also enable companies to offer card owners more customized discounts, coupons, and rewards.

Factor in further advancements like artificial intelligence (AI) and machine learning (which would allow credit cards to become smarter over time as they're fed more purchase info), and they may also soon help you plan your monthly budget as well. Using such high-tech tools, you could easily monitor and manage everyday expenses to enjoy deeper insights into your spending habits – and set up automatic alert notifications or holds if you're spending when you should be saving instead. Families may further benefit from additional high-tech upgrades as well. Imagine parental control solutions which automatically transfer over weekly allowance payments for children, track their buying patterns, and/or restrict kids to making purchases only at approved retailers up to set maximums.

Long story short: As payment technologies like blockchain solutions and cash-sharing apps continue to evolve, credit cards and other forward-thinking finance tools are rapidly transforming to keep up. But boarding buses and trains with the wave of your wrist is just the beginning for businesses looking to design customer experiences that move the needle with clients more rapidly. From fast food drive-throughs you can speed through without ever interacting with a human to convenience stores that let you grab any item and walk out without ever visiting a register (or jail), the sky's the limit here. Better still, with financial leaders around the world already working hard to make tomorrow's solutions a reality today, you won't have long to wait to cash in on these promising new innovations.

VII. ARTIFICIAL INTELLIGENCE: THE FUTURE OF BUSINESS

In a time of growing uncertainty and digital disruption, where customers increasingly expect more unique and sophisticated solutions on-demand, artificial intelligence (AI) is helping enterprises in every space optimize productivity, employ *FASTER* strategies for driving business success, and spot emerging opportunities before competitors can react. As a result, 83% of organizations now see AI-based ventures as a strategic priority for their business, according to Boston Consulting Group, with the market for these high-tech tools poised to top $190 billion worldwide by 2025. But with three quarters of commercial enterprise apps expected to leverage smart technology capabilities within the next two years, yet fewer than a quarter of organizations having currently started on their digital transformation journey, it bears reminding. The right time to start investing in self-aware initiatives capable of automating routine processes; eliminating unnecessary expenses; and analyzing, learning from, and predicting end-users' needs is right here, right now today.

"Artificial intelligence is quickly becoming a must-have if you want to stay competitive going forward," explains Gavin Day, senior vice president of technology at analytics frontrunner SAS, whose visual data mining and machine learning solutions help power smarter business decisions. "All major industries from banking to healthcare, retail, and even government are now adopting machine learning technologies. Not only do AI-powered solutions allow enterprises to better assess the data that they're collecting from end-users at every turn and transform it into actionable intelligence. These performance-enhancing technology tools also allow for major productivity and process improvements. They can help you free your people up from having to spend large amounts of time on mundane tasks and empower them to reinvest it in doing what they do best – being creative and finding smarter ways to apply business insights in context."

Just a few of the growing multitude of ways in which AI and machine learning solutions such as the custom and bespoke end-to-end offerings that vendors now provide are helping transform tomorrow's marketplace and enabling companies to increasingly adopt *FASTER* business practices include:

> • Enabling healthcare providers to quickly scan millions of medical charts and test results for anomalies or patterns of interest, and pioneer the next wave of threat prevention and treatment procedures.

- Empowering insurance companies, hospitals, and physicians to reduce the time and cost required to diagnose patients, and efficiently steer them towards optimal pathways through the care and treatment system.

- Allowing government leaders to rapidly and cost-effectively automate routine tasks (e.g. data entry and form processing), and identify areas that are ripe for process improvements, enabling faster response times and resolutions.

- Equipping emergency relief workers with crucial insights that allow them to free up limited resources for more mission-critical activities.

- Providing local governments with the tools they need to build smart cities that can self-regulate energy usage, responses to adverse weather conditions, or even the flow of everyday traffic.

- Giving traditional and online retailers a way to tailor messages and pricing strategies to individual shoppers; provide customized offers and discounts; and replace generic search and support functions with personally-contextualized conversations.

- Offering distributors more efficient ways to manage inventory stocking and fulfilment, and make smarter, more informed decisions at both the warehouse and product-aisle level.

- Helping manufacturers detect quality concern issues too minute for the human eye to see before products ever leave the factory, and apply deep learning across industrial operations to improve efficiency and output at scale.

- Making it possible for banks and financial institutions to draw upon and cross-reference multiple data sources to more rapidly assess risks, personalize customer offerings, and compellingly package services and solutions.

Given AI and process automation tools' potential to slash costs while sending profits soaring, it's no surprise that global spending on smart technology solutions is anticipated to hit $57.6 billion by 2021, per IDC. Or that 61% of organizations, regardless of size, now say that machine learning- and artificial-intelligence-related efforts will represent the most significant data initiatives that their companies will undertake within the next calendar year. Meaning that for all the unnecessary waste that AI promises to eliminate, it's also one of the most additive forces in business today. That's why eight in ten executive leaders cite it as a transformative technology that boosts productivity and creates job opportunities in addition to bolstering the bottom line.

"Three or four years ago, when I started to talking to enterprises about artificial intelligence adoption, I had to start with "what is AI, and why do you need it," notes Sudhir Jha, head of Brighterion, a Mastercard company. "Now people understand the inherent value of this technology. What they're instead struggling with today, because the promise of AI is so broad, is how to go about implementing effective solutions."

Happily, firms such as Brighterion – which provides an AI and machine learning platform that provides mission critical intelligence in real-time from any data source, regardless of scale or complexity – aren't just putting greater insights at users' fingertips than ever. They're also simplifying and speeding up the process of giving any organization a custom end-to-end smart technology upgrade. As a result, enterprises of every size can now deploy flexible, cost-effective AI rollouts and implementations, where performance, productivity, and profit gains can be measured in days, not years.

"Reliable and readymade access to high-quality data and decisioning is vital to building competitive advantage these days," explains Eliot Weinman, founder and conference chair of leading industry event AI World. "Everything is based on information now – artificial intelligence and machine learning simply draw upon this data to help augment organizations' make smarter choices. Keeping this in mind, companies are moving from a mindset where they're making investments in artificial intelligence as part of a general digital transformation play to one where they're making them as a strategic imperative."

Noting this, interest in enterprise-level automation and AI solutions (as well as potential applications for these technologies) will only continue to skyrocket in years to come, say industry insiders. "The goal is finding new ways to scale businesses, and identify additional use-cases for these advancements," seconds Brighterion's Jha. "Nowadays, companies can quickly prototype and customize AI solutions for a variety of needs, and quickly create value by doing so that's measurable in a matter of weeks, not months."

VIII. AUGMENTED AND VIRTUAL REALITY: FRESH PERSPECTIVES ON STRATEGY

Thanks to skyrocketing advancements in the fields of augmented reality (AR) and virtual reality (VR), the future of tomorrow's workplace literally lies in the eye of the beholder. Among the high-tech industry's most promising advancements, these technologies – the former of which superimposes computerized data over real-world environments, the latter of which immerses users in fully-simulated 3D landscapes – promise to reshape the enterprise environment. Moreover, with global demand expected to exceed $571.42 billion by 2025 according to Allied Market Research, countless organizations are now leveraging these tools to offer more innovative approaches to customer experience, workforce training, and product design.

"In the same way that mobile phones changed the marketplace, augmented and virtual reality solutions are set to change the way we do business in coming years," explains Michael Leone, director of commercial AR and VR at Lenovo. "From providing easier, more cost-effective ways to model buildings, computers, or cars with a wave of a hand to providing lifelike training simulations and helping field technicians scan equipment for errors at a glance using AR-enabled glasses, potential applications are endless. Solutions such as our ThinkReality platform, a combination of hardware and software tools that allow businesses to create custom AR and VR solutions on-demand, are increasingly offering a simple end-to-end way to design options for any use case that tap into their benefits."

Case in point: A large aircraft manufacturer is currently using ThinkReality's cloud-based, hardware-agnostic software platform (which works with myriad headsets) and computer-enhanced visors to scan for maintenance issues at a glance, and help on-site technicians and remote experts communicate in real-time. Likewise, a well-known biomedical company is leveraging an alternate AR headset – whose glasses can place digital pop-ups and videos atop real-world scenes – to use gesture-based and gaze-driven commands to control equipment, thereby optimizing its workflows and maximizing productivity gains. But with even more forward-thinking hardware and software solutions already in development – including mix-and-match software creation tools that let everyday users create original apps with no programming knowledge – the future only gets brighter from here. Coming applications, says Leone, will only take added advantage of 5G networks to deliver customers more sophisticated capabilities and experiences, and further cater to the unique needs of B2B solutions providers (e.g. the world's largest telecom companies) and consumer-focused organizations alike.

'The world's biggest retailers, brands, and manufacturers are already using these technologies to be more productive, and improve workers' everyday lives," explains Kris Kolo, global executive director for the VR/AR Association. "Whether encouraging communications and helping bring people together more actively, or offering more engaging news and entertainment experiences, the future is quickly taking shape as we speak."

IX. MOVING FROM ANALYTICS TO ACTION

Data is the lifeblood of any modern business. But with studies by IDC demonstrating that less than 10% of relevant information is being used to enhance organizational value, it begs the question: Why is so much of it still going untapped? Thanks to structural inefficiencies, crucial details continue to be overlooked, even as enterprises continue to collect record amounts of info. Happily, a new breed of high-tech tools is making it easier to reconcile unstructured information sources, and go from analytics to actionable business intelligence in minutes.

"Having access to the right data at the right time is crucial to getting the right answers," explains Rick Jackson, chief marketing officer of end-to-end data integration and analytics platform Qlik. "Tomorrow's business solutions shouldn't just provide organizations with easier ways to analyze opportunities from multiple dimensions. They should also use cutting-edge artificial intelligence to help them more rapidly identify what's happening in the marketplace before competitors can react. Doing so can help companies quickly move from information to insight, and create the fastest path to competitive advantage."

Multi-cloud solutions for managing data on-site or remotely like Qlik let organizations quickly surface crucial business insights at a glance. Using them, retailers can track customer behavior and social media conversations to know which products are poised to fly off shelves worldwide. Likewise, manufacturers can leverage them to more accurately predict production runs, while healthcare providers can utilize these solutions to drive more optimal patient outcomes. For example, one major chemical distribution company reduced customer churn by 59% the first year it implemented them, and one hospital system removed major performance bottlenecks in just months.

"Most people focus on analytics software's capabilities, but ignore the real challenges that prevent them from extrapolating actual value from their information – including a lack of data literacy across modern enterprises," notes Jackson. "Succeeding here isn't just about being able to do your homework – it's also about getting your workforce comfortable with the ability to analyze information."

With global research by the Data Literacy Project showing that just 24% of business leaders consider themselves data literate, and surveys by Accenture demonstrating that employees are so stressed about working with data that it costs employers $100 billion a year in lost productivity? It's clear that while many leading firms may have access to more information than ever, few are truly data-driven. "Using holistic solutions to address both technology and educational challenges, however, you can ensure that every decision is made with the most up-to-date and relevant data," says Jackson. "Doing so lets you free information from silos and help employees more rapidly translate insights into action – and additional business value."

X. MAKING TECHNOLOGY MORE HUMAN

Imagine checking into a flight just by walking on, buying groceries by nodding your head, or withdrawing funds from an ATM with a single glance. Thanks to biometric technology, which uses your voice, face, fingerprints, and other physical characteristics to securely verify your identity and control high-tech devices, you'll soon be able to do just that. Poised to be a $59.31 billion global industry by 2025 according to Grand View Research, capabilities like more rapid user identification and more intuitive shopping options are just the beginning, though. From providing better ways to fight fraud to delivering smarter customer service, a new wave of biometrics providers are not only currently expanding the many futuristic applications this technology can be put to by leaps and bounds. They're also revolutionizing entire industries' ability to leverage *FASTER*, more forward-thinking business solutions and pioneering a host of new ways to make every high-tech interaction more human.

"The future of business lies in highly-intelligent and -automated transactions and smart, seamless customer interaction," explains Brett Beranek, General Manager of Security and Biometrics at Nuance Communications. "Among today's fastest-growing trends, the push towards more natural and personalized exchanges is quickly making biometrics a go-to technology for firms all around the world, including Fortune 500 leaders." Not only do biometrics offer a faster and more foolproof means of accessing electronic devices and physical locations than PIN numbers and keycards, proponents of these technologies argue. With 67% of respondents to IBM Security's Future of Identity study stating that they're comfortable using biometric authentication methods at present, and 87% looking forward to using these technologies in the very near future? You can be certain that such high-tech advancements (including voice-, palm-, and retina-scanning tools and more) will only become more of a preferred solution for a growing range of global industries from healthcare to finance with each passing year.

Sample tools such as the fingerprint scanners and facial recognition systems that millions currently use to unlock or manipulate smartphones and tablets with ease are just the tip of the iceberg, however. Today's leading biometrics solutions aren't just capable of detecting surface characteristics such as the sound or tone of your voice. They're also capable of learning your speaking, typing, texting, and behavioral patterns, as well as memorizing your preferred vocabulary – and predicting when someone is trying to impersonate you on the phone or during digital transactions of every kind. As a result, many biometrics technologies now make it possible to create unique "voiceprints" and "eyeprints" (similar to fingerprints) that are incredibly easy to use, can't be faked, and allow users to maintain persistent digital identities wherever they go.

Biometrics solutions presently currently serve over 400 million customers worldwide, and have already saved many industry-leading finance, telecommunications, and insurance companies over $1 billion just in fraud prevention alone. Likewise, marketing and retail leaders of every kind are increasingly using biometrics tools to create competitive advantage by quickly recognizing individual shoppers, and crafting customized offers or solutions to them. But these technologies, which also have the potential to radically boost organizational productivity and performance, don't just have immediate benefits on the front-end of the commercial spectrum as well. They're also increasingly being deployed to cut costs and streamline back-end operations by numerous public and private institutions, including top government agencies, around the world as well.

Take, for instance, Iris ID's cutting-edge suite of hardware and software solutions, which is capable of identifying users based on scans of their irises. (Which are unique to every individual.) Not only are these tools – able to be quickly customized for virtually any application or regulatory environment – growingly being used by to expedite security checks and travel at a range of leading airports worldwide. They're also being used by an increasing range of healthcare providers to authenticate and track patients as they move through care pathways, and ensure that the right medicine and treatment are provided at the right time every step of the way. Likewise, these tools are also being deployed on farms and production facilities around the world to help supervisors track workers' hours as they move about corporate campuses and factory floors of every kind. In addition to being more reliable and trusted than alternate methods of authentication, biometrics solutions – which require only the use of users' bodies to function – are also more amenable and accessible to audiences of all backgrounds.

"Traditional identification tools such as access cards and hardware devices aren't particularly reliable, user-friendly, or convenient," says Mohammed Murad, VP of Global Sales, Marketing, and Business

Development for Iris ID. "Like facial scanning, they also come with many negative privacy connotations attached. Instead, biometrics technologies provide secure, cost-affordable, and easily-integratable solutions that employees feel comfortable opting into using." Unsurprisingly, market leaders in every field are capitalizing on Iris ID's tools to deliver next-gen solutions in an unprecedented range of forms. Sample uses include creating security checkpoints that limit access to highly-classified areas such as data centers and R&D labs at the globe's leading high-tech firms; providing easy, contactless access to workstations and equipment for pharmaceutical and laboratory technicians in every field; and making it possible for government agencies to dispense documentation and passports to travelers from high-tech kiosks on-demand.

But with studies suggesting that eight in ten customers are actively seeking more opportunities to tap into the potential of biometrics, and that nearly 90% of businesses will be using these technologies within the next year? Even these forward-thinking applications are just the tip of the iceberg. Among the many new types of *FASTER*, more forward-thinking innovations you can expect to see biometrics enabling in the very near future are:

• Entire countries whose healthcare or government ID systems never require the use of printed documents or written records to verify and serve citizens.

• Online retailers that make it possible to buy the season's hottest steals and deals in seconds just by talking to your TV or computer.

• Pharmacies that can dispense prescriptions and medicine without ever demanding that you interact with a human technician.

• Bank machines that you can withdraw cash, make payments, and perform transactions from just by looking at their screens, without the need to carry a debit card or PIN number around for safety.

• Customer support hotlines that can predict your needs the second that you call into them, and provide personalized answers and solutions, without having to wait on hold.

• Workplaces where you'll never have to check in with a supervisor, or worry about verifying overtime billings, because computerized systems will know exactly when you've clocked in and out.

• Stadiums, concert halls, and public spaces that won't require you to bring tickets, because they'll know at a glance if you've already purchased a seat for the evening's performance.

• A world where you won't need a passport, because airport security personnel will already know everything they need about your travels.

• Home, car, and garage doors that will recognize you as you approach and unlock without a single turn of a key.

• Banks that can intelligently detect and identify thieves trying to steal your hard-earned cash – and automatically report these individuals to the appropriate authorities.

Just ask Jeff Maynard, CEO and founder of Biometric Signature ID, which is reinventing the humble password and radically improving organizations' ability to fight cybercrime using technologies that verify individuals by asking them to draw numbers or letters on virtually any device. (And whose solutions now enable hundreds of universities, mortgage lenders, and healthcare providers to accurately determine who's submitting forms and attempting to access online data.) "From helping colleges make sure that students are doing their own homework to healthcare providers confirm who's looking to obtain personal information, potential uses for the technology are enormous," he says. "Whether you're talking about verifying purchases in virtual reality and gaming applications or finding better ways to prevent organizations from falling victim to data breaches, the future clearly lies in biometrics."

>>BRINGING IT TOGETHER:

10 WAYS TO BECOME A POWERHOUSE OF GROWTH AND INNOVATION

In the end, just how powerful a tool for driving forward motion can thinking *FASTER* be? Just ask one of the world's most successful business leaders.

Case in point: Since its humble origins as an online bookseller that debuted out of founder Jeff Bezos' garage in 1994, online retail giant Amazon.com has grown to become a category leader in dozens of high-tech spaces. Over 25 years later, a firm that was generating $20,000 a week in sales within 30 days of its inception has exploded to become a $280 billion corporate titan with a fast-growing footprint in consumer devices, cloud computing, and streaming media, among dozens of other spaces. But according to innovation adviser John Rossman, a former executive who helped launch and scale the firm's marketplace business, the secret to the company's history-making success is simpler than most would suspect.

"Becoming a digital leader isn't just about becoming speedier (efficient at staying in motion) or more agile (able to create change)," he says. "Rather, it's also about striving to achieve operational excellence, and always striving to raise the bar, at every turn." As Rossman explains in recent book *Think Like Amazon: 50 ½ Ideas to Become a Digital Leader*, finding ways to successfully innovate, explore new markets, and spark business growth doesn't have to be time-consuming or difficult either when you just make a point to apply a few forward-looking shifts in strategy and thinking.

Promote a customer-focused obsession in your business. "When you're truly obsessed with raising the bar for customers, it doesn't just become your #1 priority – it also becomes your #2 and #3 priorities as well," chuckles Rossman. "Most companies pay the idea lip service. But when you're truly obsessed with the topic, it means that you're spending an amount of time, effort, and energy pursuing it that appears strange to others." Amazon, he says, frequently pushes itself hard and expends seemingly exorbitant amounts of effort and capital to improve the shopping, returns, and customer service experiences for its shoppers. But it also uses this singular level of focus to innovate to a degree that almost seems irresponsible to rivals, who often balk at the time and cost required to achieve business breakthroughs and puzzle through difficult strategic challenges, inadvertently leaving

Amazon to reap the rewards. "If you think back, in the year 2000, the company announced everyday free shipping to the industry – and the industry's response was that it was ridiculous and unsustainable," Rossman reminds. "But today, thanks to Amazon's singular level of customer focus, it's become the everyday norm."

Start with well-defined metrics, then strive to exceed expectations. Many digital businesses hold their computer and IT systems to strict performance and uptime metrics. When it comes to providing top-notch service, says Rossman, Amazon also challenges its staff to work towards maintaining and exceeding similar well-defined and measurable goals in terms of its delivery performance, turnaround times, and overall customer satisfaction. For example, says Rossman, the firm is always working to reduce friction (e.g. the number of action steps necessary to make a purchase or process a refund) and pain points for its customers, as well as striving to improve its supply chain logistics. "Consider how easy Amazon makes it to obtain a refund on your purchases," he suggests. "If you think about it, it's counter-intuitive – most companies don't want to make it easier for customers to get their money back. But Amazon instead takes the long-term view that if customers are happier, they'll make more purchases. One of my favorite new concepts is the ability to return an item purchased online to an Amazon bookstore or Kohl's outlet without even needing to bring the box or receipt. You just hand off the item and it's gone... Yet another way the company is working to surprise, delight, and go well beyond customers' expectations."

Provide platforms that allow you to capitalize on user-generated and third-party content to create exponential growth. "It's important to provide tools and incentives that encourage other actors in your organization's ecosystem (e.g. customers or sellers) to help tackle hard challenges on your behalf," explains Rossman. "Or, in other words, to capitalize on OPW – other people's work. You could argue that, to a degree, from the way it leverages customer reviews to third-party sellers' product information and inventory readouts, the entire Amazon marketplace has been built on the back of this strategy." To make this business strategy work though, he says, three core pillars need to be place. You need to: (1) Provide a well-thought-out incentive system to encourage others' participation (2) offer powerful, user-friendly tools that can help them and (3) make sure you're effectively governing these systems and solutions to offer the best user experience possible.

Eliminate hierarchy so that you can fast-track decision-making and kick internal roadblocks to the curb. "I truly believe that Jeff Bezos' #1 concern when it comes to Amazon isn't supply chain disruption, government regulation, or outside interference, but bureaucracy," notes Rossman. "He's always worked hard to promote entrepreneurial thinking and speed up internal activity where possible, and makes a point at every turn to promote a sense of urgency in the business." In fact, says Rossman, Amazon is famous for its focus on "two-pizza" teams (which are up to 10 people in size – no bigger than two pizzas will feed) who retain complete end-to-end ownership of core business features and capabilities. From the company's online imaging and cloud computing services to its item return process, he explains, two-pizza teams have helped craft some of Amazon's most defining features. This approach – which allows members of these teams to enjoy more autonomy, accountability, and ownership of any business function – increases the firm's agility and ability to make decisions on a dime, Rossman explains. "When you have a small team that's in charge of a feature or capability, and completely focused and obsessed with creating world-class experiences," he says, "then the service they're powering becomes more nimble, more scalable, and more focused."

Create simple, well-defined processes that are capable of working at scale. Many organizations see the idea of "process" an excuse for letting bureaucracy fester. But according to Rossman, Amazon's view is that well-designed processes aren't just easily understood and manageable. They also help you keep red tape to a minimum. Developing them begins, he says, by giving these processes a simple name ("inventory management process," "sales tracking process," etc.) that all key stakeholders can recognize. Then it continues by ensuring that all processes follow an interchangeable model with a well-defined scope and setup, so they're easy to get one's head around, and responsibility for managing them lies with an individual or team everyone knows to call on. Well-designed processes are further supported by a host of day-to-day and long-range metrics, he seconds, and a working roadmap of new ideas and capabilities that teams can implement in the future to enhance these processes over time.

Take a more objective approach to hiring. Every modern organization is competing to attract top talent today. But fundamental hiring mistakes often occur when firms are in a rush to fill positions, Rossman says, which can lead to lasting problems, especially if candidates lack the skill set or adaptability needed to evolve as market realities and job responsibilities shift over time.

To avoid these challenges, every open position at Amazon isn't just assigned a hiring committee, but also a "bar-raiser" – a member of the hiring committee who hails from a different department and group than the team to which the new hire will be assigned. This objective observer (who remains removed from team politics, and has the power to veto decisions) not only works to prevent manager bias, and keep the company from hiring mistakes made in haste. They also make a point to screen candidates to ensure that they exhibit the values and principles that Amazon promotes on the job, and bring skills to the table that are adaptable to future scenarios, noting that job responsibilities frequently evolve over time.

Avoid getting comfortable and creating a cushy, country club type environment across your organization. No matter how well your business does, or how big it becomes, it's important to stay hungry, even when you're successful, Rossman asserts. If you're not constantly looking for ways to step up your game, or experimenting with new solutions, like Amazon does, you're selling yourself short, he says, and sub-optimizing your team's potential. "I remember a meeting with Bezos where he turned in the direction of Microsoft's campus and said that if we [became a country club like them], we'd be dead in the water," Rossman chuckles. "The point being that even if you're doing well in the marketplace, you always have to work hard and not hold back to ensure that you and your staff are creating a future that's every bright as the one you may have inherited."

Don't let anxiety get you so hung up that you can't make decisions. Amazon is always working to help employees make better decisions faster, says Rossman. Part of the way it does so is by framing them around the concept of one-way and two-way doors. "A one-way-door decision – similar to getting married – is one that's really difficult and expensive decision to undo," he explains. "On the other hand, two-way-door decisions are those smaller, less permanent choices you make that you can test, revise, and (if you need to) sometimes put down and come back to later. It turns out that most decisions are two-way-door decisions. As business leaders, we just tend to overestimate the importance or impact of them many times, and escalate them up the corporate ladder or delay or pass the buck on decision-making as a result. A better approach to tackling them is instead to break these two-way-door decisions up into smaller step-by-step choices, and to get better about coming up with ways that we can quickly- and cost-affordably experiment with different approaches to problem-solving." A decision is just a type of hypothesis, he reminds: If you're uncertain about which choice to make when making a decision, the best thing you can do is figure out how to test your theories quickly and cheaply, learn something from them, and rapidly pivot, adapt, or move along based on the feedback received.

Write down and clearly articulate a plan for new ideas and innovations on paper before electing to move forward with them. At Amazon, no major new initiative is undertaken until employees write out a six-page document proposing new business ideas or opportunities, which then undergoes extensive management review. By forcing workers to create comprehensive and well-defined narratives, Rossman says, the exercise challenges them to think more critically about various concepts and improve ideas' overall focus. In addition, those crafting these proposals are also challenge to write out future-facing press releases and FAQ (frequently asked question) documents, that imagine what these solutions will ultimately look like and the core function that they will serve, and define metrics by which their performance will be gauged. Because the process encourages submitters to vet ideas extensively from a conceptual standpoint before actual hands-on testing occurs, it ultimately allows the company save on time and resources that would otherwise be spent pursuing these learnings. It's only after concepts have made their way to print, and undergone extensive discussion and debate, that they float up to a team that decides which ventures deserve to be funded and which need retooling. "Amazon spends a lot of time writing, debating, and reviewing future plans," says Rossman. "Going through this process creates a disciplined approach to strategic planning that also helps the company maintain its focus and avoid wasting resources spinning its wheels in less-productive directions."

Apply structured methods for governing all forms of innovation in your business. "At business events, I like to poll groups of executive leaders," says Rossman. "When I ask them how many feel that it's important for their companies to be more innovative, entire roomfuls of hands shoot up. But when I ask who has a structured methodology in place for managing this process, and the process of strategic experimentation with new ideas that's necessary to support it, virtually all of those hands drop." To successfully juggle the process of innovation, he says, it's not enough to generate ideas alone. You also need to have a formal process in place that lets you manage speculative and incremental innovations by engaging in quick-hit learning experiments, capturing these learnings, and rapidly applying them to future tests. And, on the flip side, one for managing larger, more traditional projects as well that takes an opposite route, allowing you to systematically de-risk ventures and take a more disciplined approach to decision-making as you pursue a holistic portfolio of strategic innovations.

INNOVATION IS SIMPLER THAN YOU THINK

Ultimately though, as much as Amazon champions these principles, don't be fooled, says Rossman. Building and maintaining competitive advantage going forward isn't about having to think like any one single organization, he asserts. Rather, he says, it's about taking a larger, more comprehensive view on future-proofing yourself and building competitive advantage, and asking yourself what you and your organization are willing to do differently to achieve better results.

"Finding ways to get ahead more frequently in tomorrow's digital world is simply about finding ways to get in the practice of exercising better business habits," he points out. "It's about asking yourself what new skills you're willing to invest in, what new efforts you're willing to pursue, and what you're willing to work hard at and constantly improve upon in order to get the same results that Amazon gets. On the bright side, as much effort as staying ahead of the curve takes, as you can see, the results speak for themselves…"

>>>> CREATING A BETTER FUTURE FASTER >>>>

There you have it: A simpler, *FASTER* formula for getting things done – as well as dozens of examples of ways you can design or redesign leadership, workforce, and business strategies to better help put you and your organization on the fast-track to success. Our ability to create positive results is a direct result of the mindset we choose to apply when weighing and considering any given challenge. Want to instantly boost your business or career prospects? Change the lens through which you choose to look at the world and you can quickly change your fortunes.

I'd love to hear more about how you are implementing these strategies in your workplace and career. Please feel free to reach out at www.AKeynoteSpeaker.com with your thoughts anytime, or follow us on Facebook, LinkedIn, or Twitter (@akeynotespeaker) to pick up even more insights on how to steer your business towards a brighter future. I look forward to learning more about the methodologies and solutions you're using to stay ahead of the curve – and how you're leveraging them to create positive results in life and business at every turn.

-Scott Steinberg

ACKNOWLEDGEMENTS

BOB, TIM, NEIL, PETE, MIKE, STEPHANE, SUE, SANDEEP, TAMARA, ERIC, AND JEAN – THANKS FOR ALL THE LATE NIGHTS AND PROFOUND INSIGHTS. THIS IS A FAR BETTER WORK FOR YOUR THOUGHTS AND PERSPECTIVES.

ABOUT THE AUTHOR

Hailed as The Master of Innovation by Fortune magazine, and the World's Leading Business Strategist, award-winning professional speaker Scott Steinberg is among today's best-known trends experts and futurists. A strategic adviser to four-star generals, government leaders, and a who's-who of Fortune 500s, he's helped craft dozens of business strategies and product designs for the world's top brands, and is the bestselling author of 14 books including Make Change Work for You: 10 Ways to Future-Proof Yourself, Fearlessly Innovate, and Succeed Despite Uncertainty, The Business Etiquette Bible, and Millennial Marketing: Bridging the Generation Gap. The President and CEO of BIZDEV: The Intl. Association for Business Development and Strategic Planning™ and founder of critically-acclaimed travel + lifestyle trends magazine SELECT: Your City's Secrets Unlocked™, his website is www.AKeynoteSpeaker.com. Named one of America's top futurists by the BBC and a "top trendsetter to follow" by the Fortune 500, this leading business insider and analyst has covered consumer, business, and lifestyle trends for 600+ outlets from CNN to Rolling Stone.

ABOUT THE EDITOR

Damon Brown (www.damonbrown.net) helps side hustlers, solopreneurs, and other non-traditional creatives bloom. He co-founded the popular platonic connection app Cuddlr and led it to acquisition within a year, all while being the primary caretaker of his infant first son. He now guides others through his consulting, daily Inc. Magazine column at www.incdamonbrown.com, and public speaking at TED and other platforms. Damon's latest book is Bring Your Worth: Level Up Your Creative Power, Value & Service to the World, the follow-up to his best-seller The Ultimate Bite-Sized Entrepreneur: 76 Ways to Boost Time, Focus & Productivity on Your Big Idea. Join the conversation and get your free creative entrepreneurship tools at JoinDamon.me.

www.ingramcontent.com/pod-product-compliance
Lightning Source LLC
Chambersburg PA
CBHW021417210526
45463CB00001B/419